Sudbury Ontario in Colour Photos, Saving Our History One Photo at a Time

Photography by Barbara Raué
©2018

Series Name: Cruising Ontario

Book 216: Sudbury

Cover photo: 80 Elm Street, Page 35

©All the photos in this book have been taken with my cameras. I own the rights to them.

Series Name: Cruising Ontario
Saving Our History One Photo at a Time
in colour photos

Books Available in Alphabetical Order:
Aberfoyle, Acton, Ajax, Alton, Amherstburg, Ancaster, Arthur, Auburn, Aylmer, Ayr, Beaver Valley, Belgrave, Belleville, Bloomingdale, Blyth, Brantford, Brockville, Burford, Burlington, Caledon, Caledonia, Cambridge, Carlow, Chatsworth, Clifford, Collingwood, Conestogo, Delhi, Dorchester to Aylmer, Drayton, Drumbo, Dundas, Dunlop, Eden Mills, Elmira, Elora, Erin, Essex, Fergus, Goderich, Grimsby, Guelph, Hagersville, Hamilton, Hanover, Harriston, Hespeler, Jarvis, Kingston, Kingsville, Kitchener, Lake Superior, Lincoln, Linwood, Listowel, London, Lucknow, Merrickville, Mono, Mount Forest, Mount Pleasant, Neustadt, New Hamburg, Newboro, Newport, Niagara-on-the-Lake, Niagara Falls, North Bay, Oakville, Onondaga, Orangeville, Orillia, Oshawa, Owen Sound, Palmerston, Paris, Pelham, Perth, Peterborough, Petrolia, Pickering, Port Colborne, Port Elgin, Portland, Preston, Rockwood, Sarnia, Sault Ste. Marie, Seaforth, Sheffield, Shelburne, Simcoe, Smiths Falls, Smithville, Southampton, St. Catharines, St. George, St. Jacobs, St. Marys, St. Thomas, Stoney Creek, Stratford, Thamesford, Thunder Bay, Tillsonburg, Toronto, Waterdown, Waterford, Waterloo, Welland, Wellesley, West Flamborough, Westport, Whitby, Windsor, Wingham, Woodstock

Book 204-206: Oshawa
Book 207-209: Niagara Falls
Book 210: North Bay
Book 211: Fort Erie

Book 212-215: Haldimand County
Book 216: Sudbury

Table of Contents

The Big Nickel	Page 6
Beech Street	Page 23
Ste. Anne Road	Page 25
Elgin Street	Page 28
Elm Street	Page 34
Durham Street	Page 37
Larch Street	Page 41
Lisgar Street	Page 43
Cedar Street	Page 44
Frood Road	Page 46
Pearl Street Water Tower	Page 48
Paris Street	Page 49
St. Charles Street	Page 50
Notre Dame Street	Page 53
Rink Street Super stack	Page 55
Science North	Page 56
Onaping High Falls	Page 61

Greater Sudbury is the largest city in Northern Ontario. Sudbury was founded in 1883 following the discovery of nickel ore during the construction of the transcontinental railway. The people live in an urban core and many smaller communities scattered around three hundred lakes and among hills of rock blackened by smelting activity. Mining and related industries dominated the economy for much of the twentieth century. The two major mining companies which shaped the history of Sudbury were Inco, now Vale Limited, which employed more than 25% of the population by the 1970s, and Falconbridge, now Glencore. Sudbury has since expanded from its resource-based economy to emerge as the major retail, economic, health and educational centre for North-eastern Ontario.

The city recovered from the Great Depression much more quickly than almost any other city in North America due to increased demand for nickel in the 1930s. Sudbury was the fastest-growing city and one of the wealthiest cities in Canada for most of the decade. Many of the city's social problems in the Great Depression era were caused by the difficulty in keeping up with all of the new infrastructure demands created by rapid growth. Employed mineworkers sometimes ended up living in boarding houses or makeshift shanty towns because demand for new housing was rising faster than supply.

The open coke beds used in the early to mid-twentieth century and logging for fuel resulted in almost a total loss of native vegetation in the area. Consequently, the terrain was made up of exposed rocky outcrops permanently stained charcoal black, first by the air pollution from the roasting yards. Acid rain added more staining, in a layer that penetrates up to three inches into the once pink-grey granite.

The construction of the Inco Super stack in 1972 dispersed sulphuric acid through the air over a much wider area, reducing the acidity of local precipitation. This enabled the city to begin an environmental recovery program. In the late 1970s, private and public interests combined to establish a "regreening" effort. Lime was spread over the charred soil by hand and by aircraft. Seeds of wild grasses and other vegetation were also spread. More than nine million new trees have been planted in the city.

Sudbury's pentlandite, pyrite and pyrrhotite ores contain profitable amounts of many elements — primarily nickel and copper, but also platinum, palladium and other valuable metals.

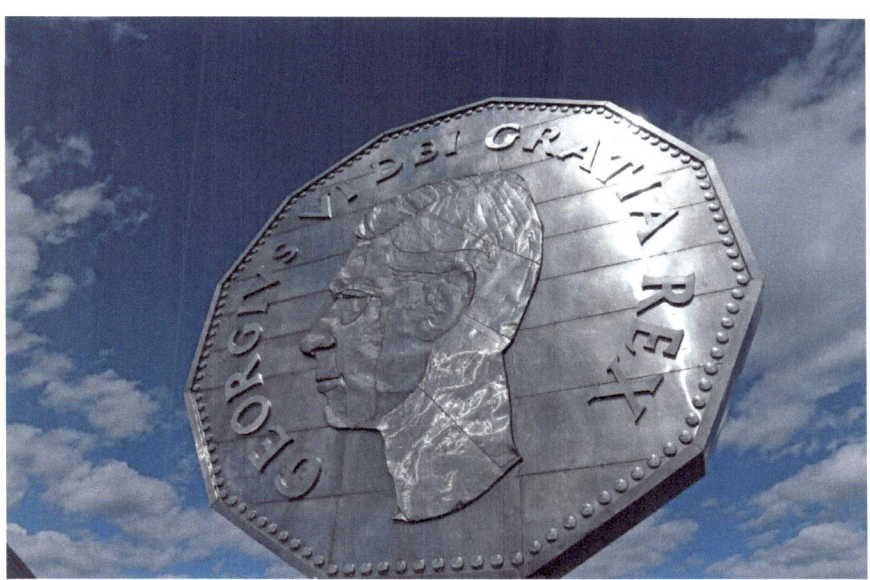

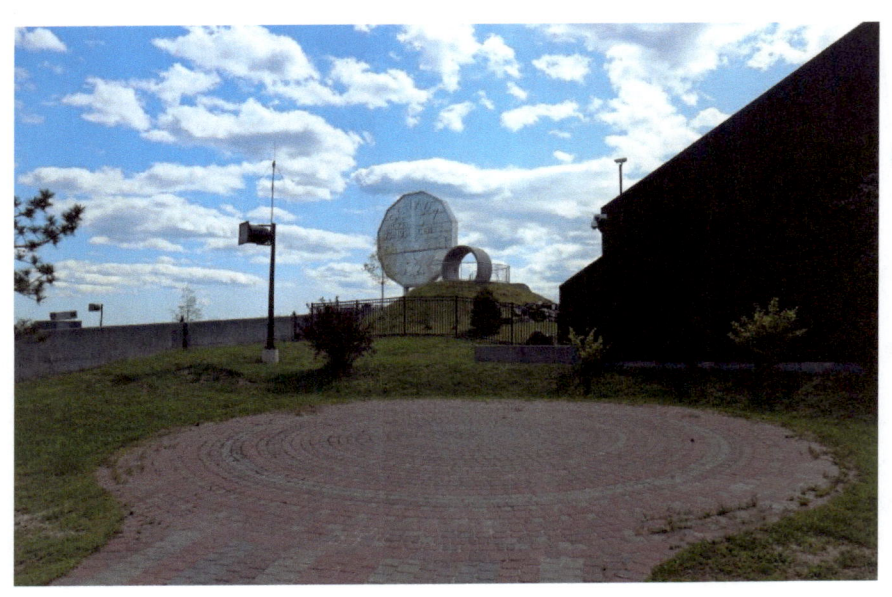

122 Big Nickel Road – Dynamic Earth

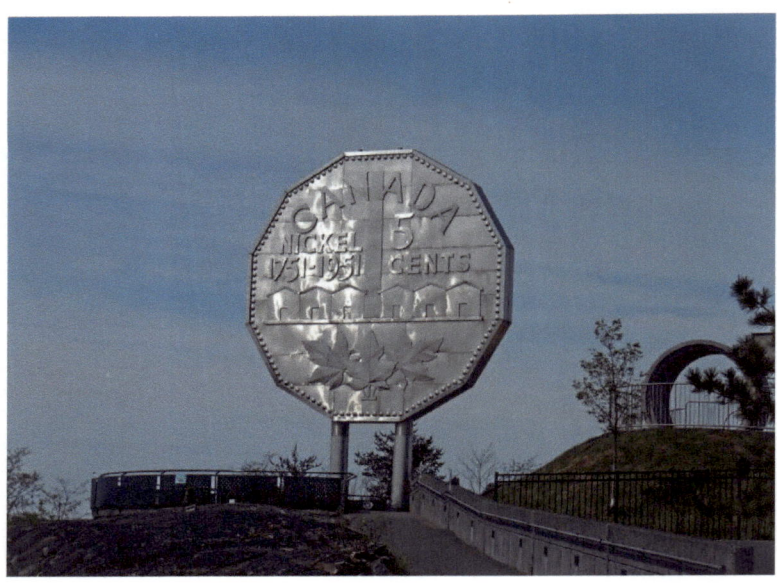

Dr. Ted Szilva was the creator of the Canadian Centennial Numismatic Park which opened on July 22, 1964. Ted spearheaded the creation of the Big Nickel and the original Big Nickel mine on the Dynamic Earth site. Today, the Big Nickel is an icon synonymous with Sudbury, the nickel capital of the world.

In 1949 the Bank of Canada launched a nationwide contest for the design of the 1951 five-cent coin to mark the bicentennial of the chemical isolation of nickel by the Swedish chemist Baron Axel Frederic Cronstedt.

The Big Nickel is a replica of this commemorative 12-sided coin designed by Stephen Trenka. The obverse features King George VI who was the monarch at the time. The reverse features a stylized nickel refinery with one large smokestack. It weighs almost 13,000 kilograms and is nine meters in diameter.

Scientists and residents of Greater Sudbury work hand in hand to innovate and implement new strategies to re-green the community. The City of Greater Sudbury is a world leader in reclamation of environmentally impacted landscapes.

The main components of Sudbury's ore are nickel, copper and sulphur. Early methods of smelting released a lot of sulphur dioxide gas (SO_2) into the atmosphere. Since the early 1970s, SO_2 has been greatly reduced which has fostered ecological recovery. In 2015, healthy, reproducing small mouth bass returned to Sudbury's Clearwater Lake which is slowly recovering from acidification.

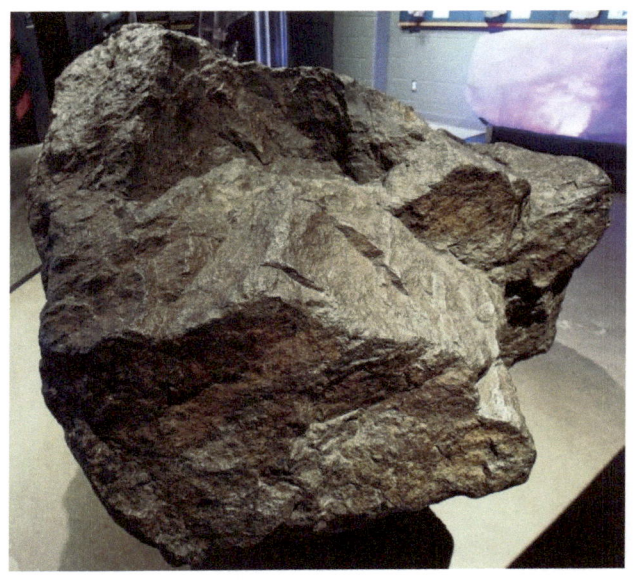

This sample of Sudbury ore weighs 4,105 kilograms. It contains about 4% nickel, 3% copper, .13% cobalt, and small amounts or precious metals including silver, gold, platinum, palladium, ruthenium, rhodium, and iridium. There is enough nickel and copper in this sample to make 33,400 two-dollar coin rings and 500 meters of copper pipe.

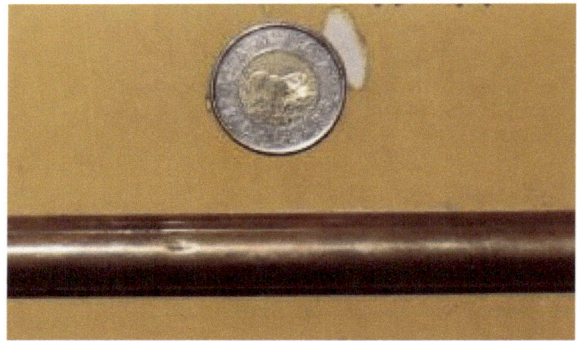

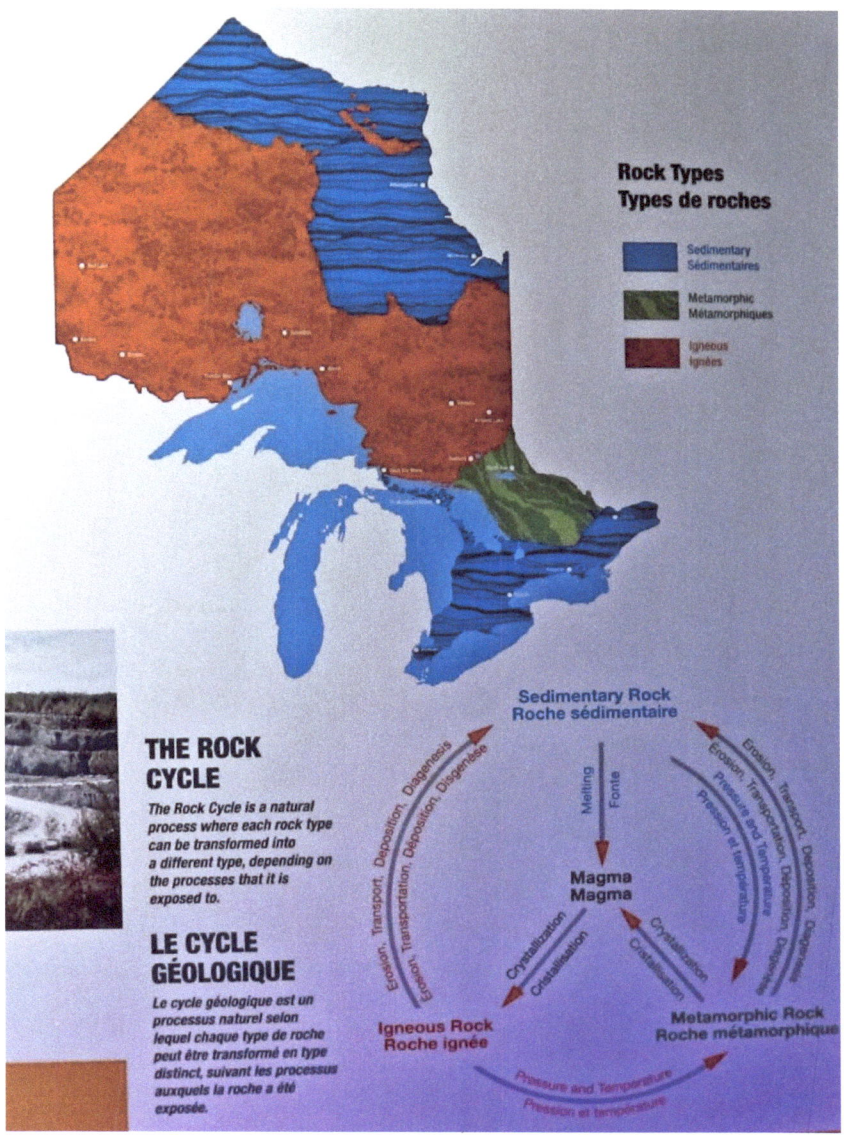

Ontario Quarries – Quarries are open pit mines where bedrock is removed for use in the construction industry, as aggregate or as dimension stone. The rock cycle is a natural process where each rock type can be transformed into a different type depending on the processes it is exposed to.

Igneous rocks form when molten rock cools. Much of Ontario is made up of igneous formations. Granite is the most commonly quarried igneous rock in Ontario.

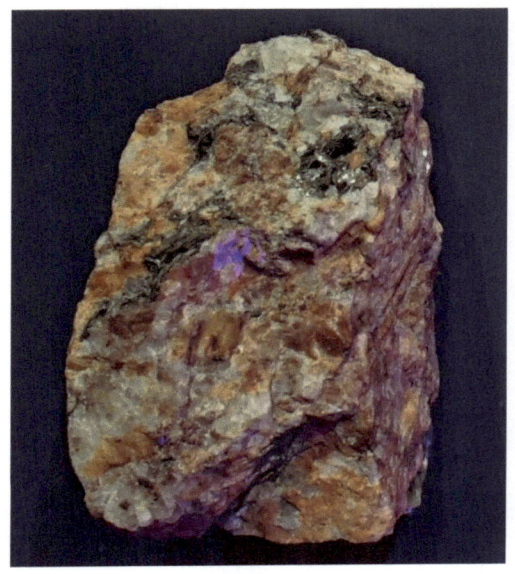

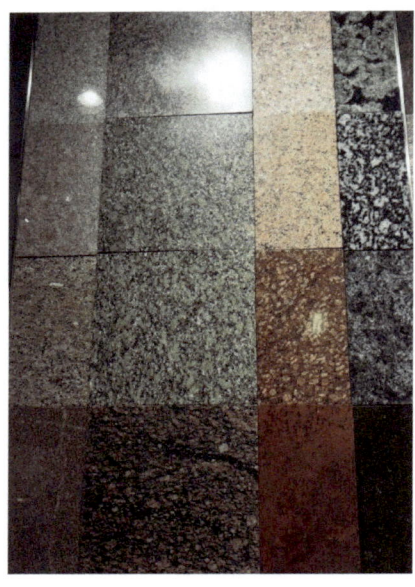

Metamorphic rocks are created when rock is exposed to high heat and pressure. This is the least common type of rock in Ontario. In Ontario, mostly metamorphic gneiss and marble are quarried.

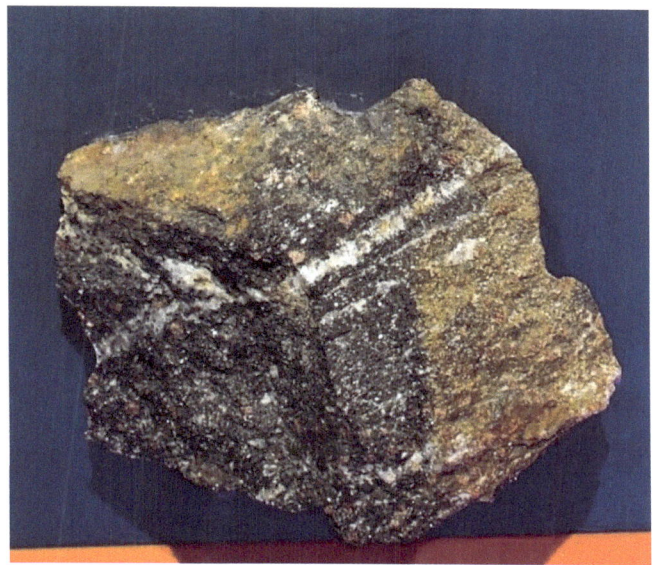

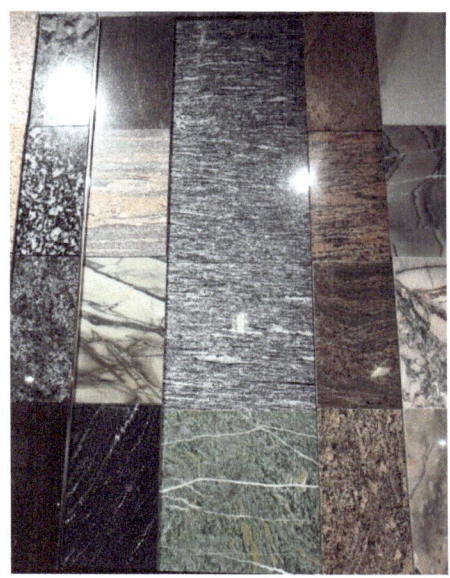

Sedimentary rocks form when sediments are deposited by water or air. This sample of fossiliferous limestone is a type of sedimentary rock quarried locally on Manitoulin Island.

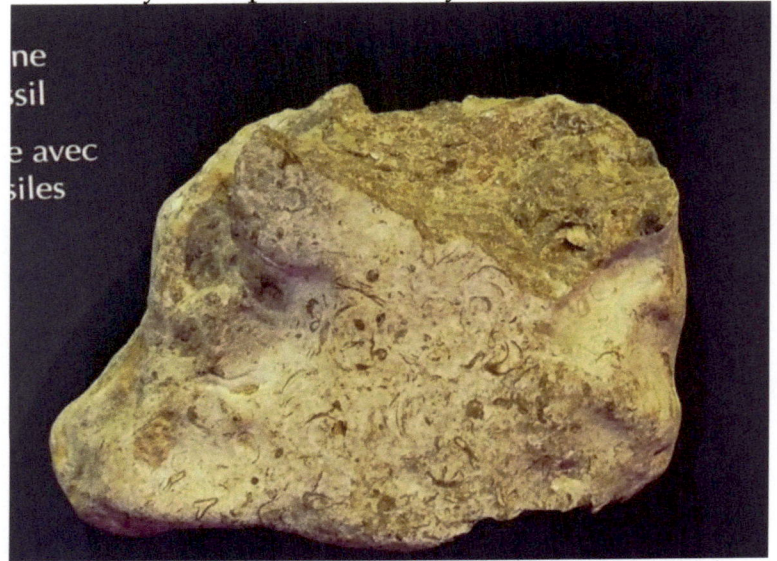

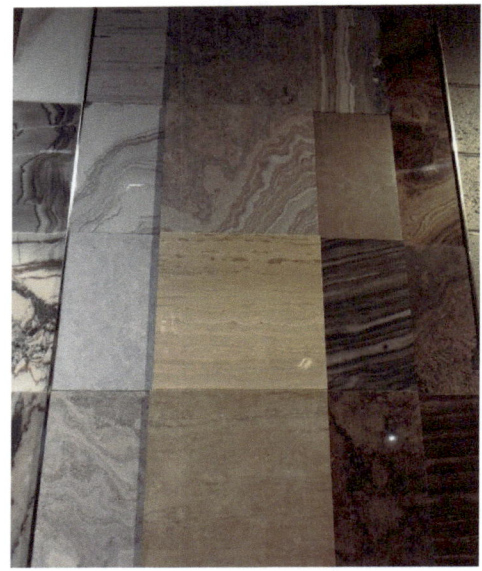

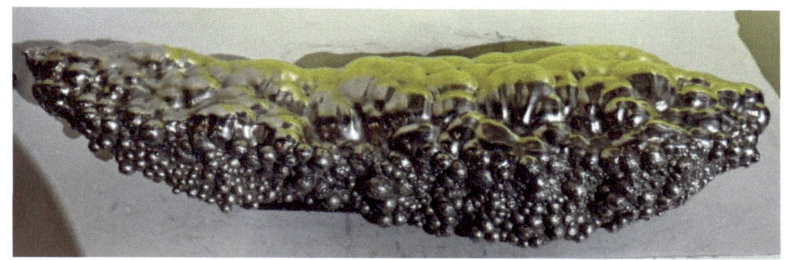

Refined Nickel – 99.9% Free

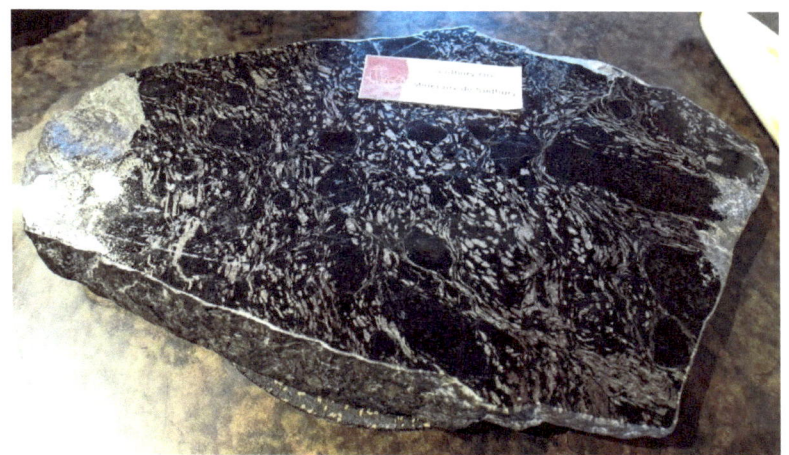

Sudbury ore

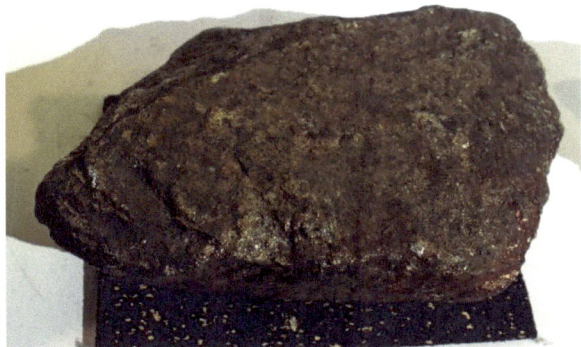

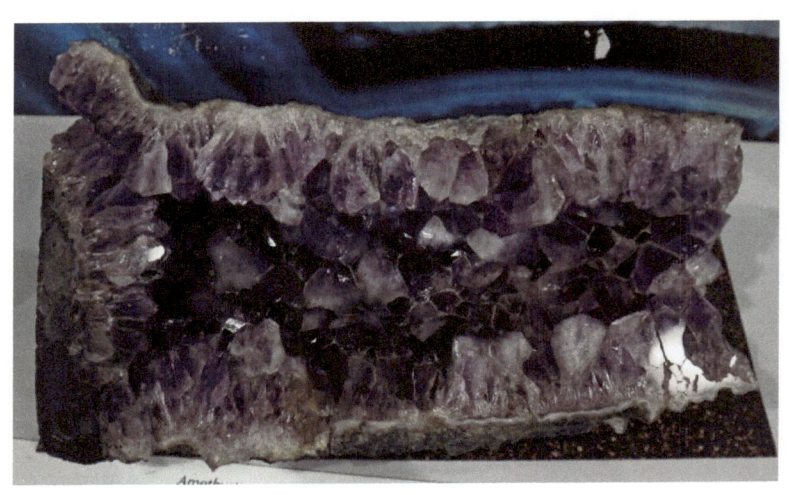

Amethyst

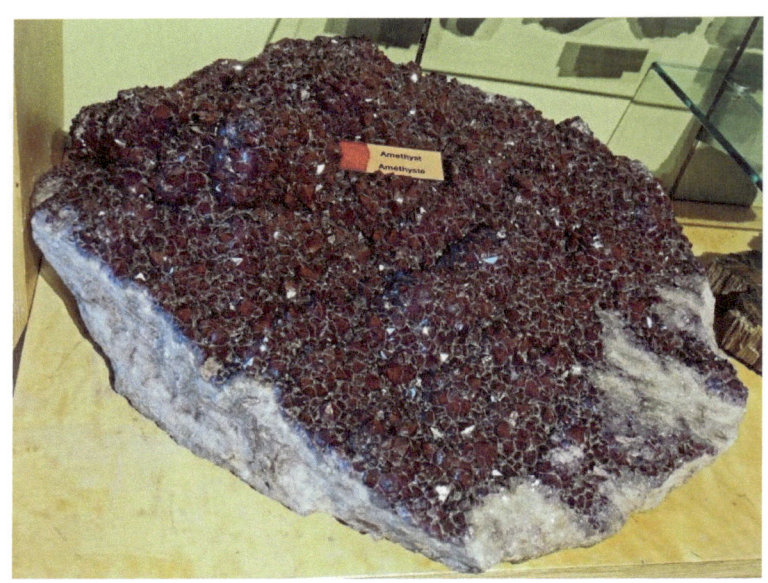

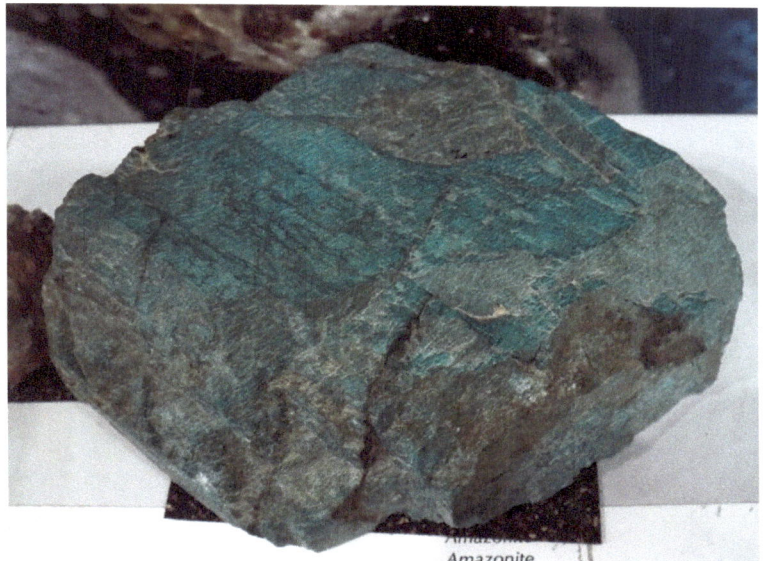
Amazonite

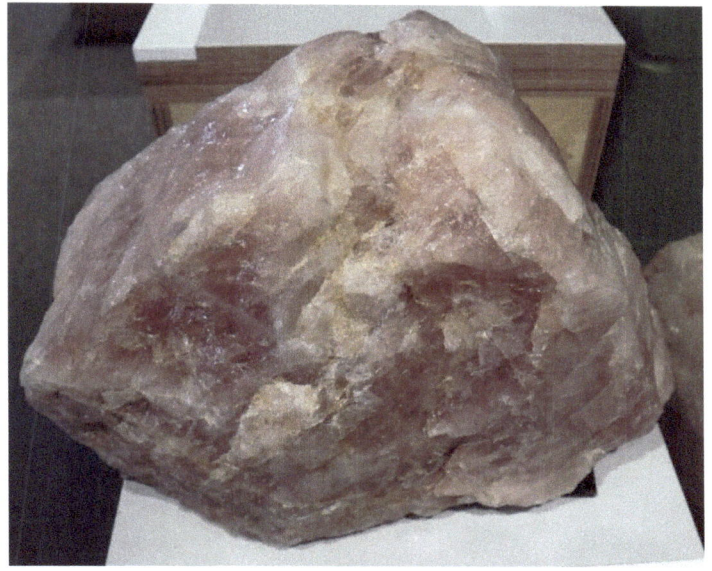
Rose Quartz

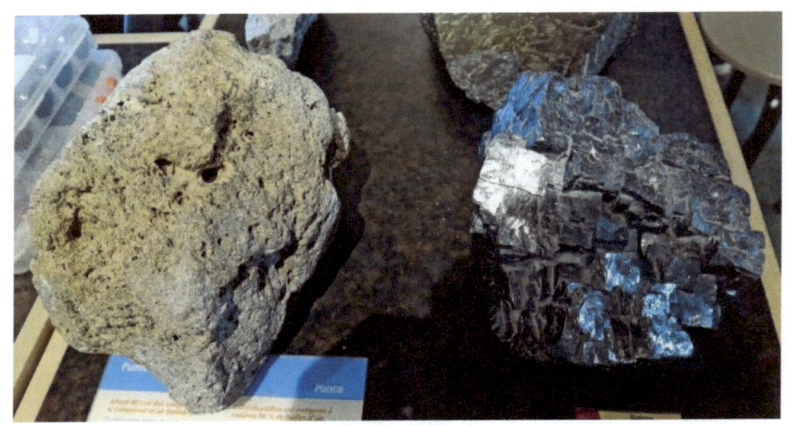

Ponce and Galena

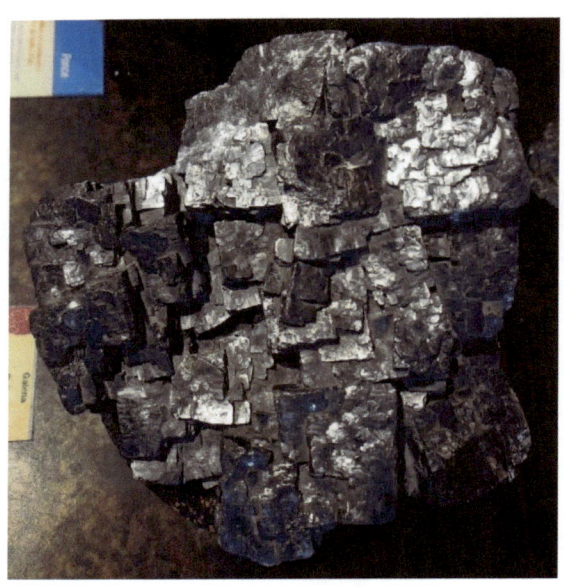

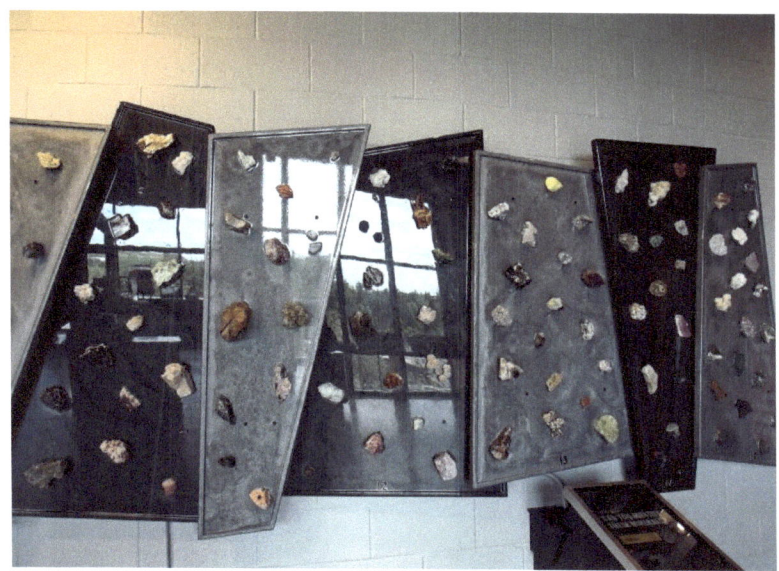

Wall of Minerals

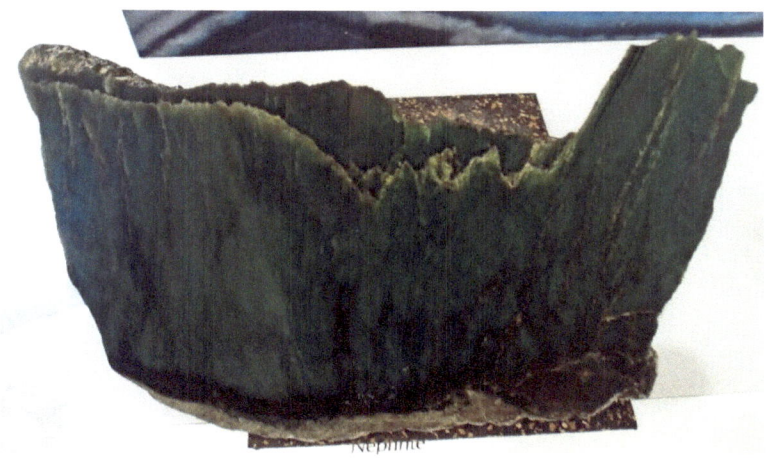

Nephrite

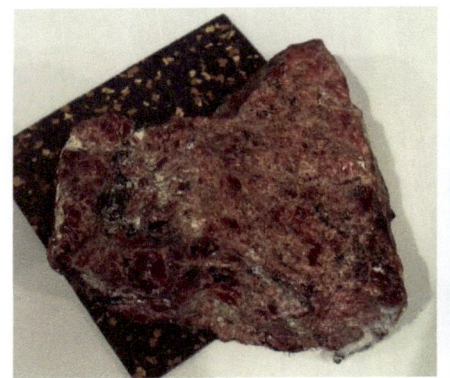
Eudialyte

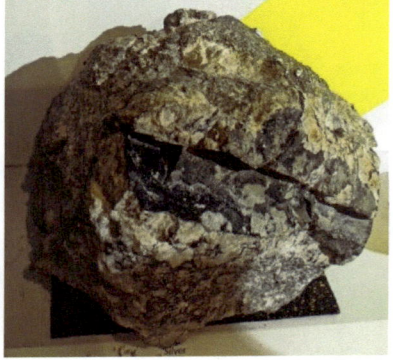
Silver

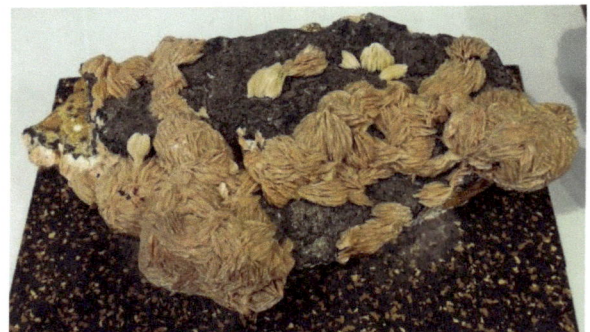
Barite

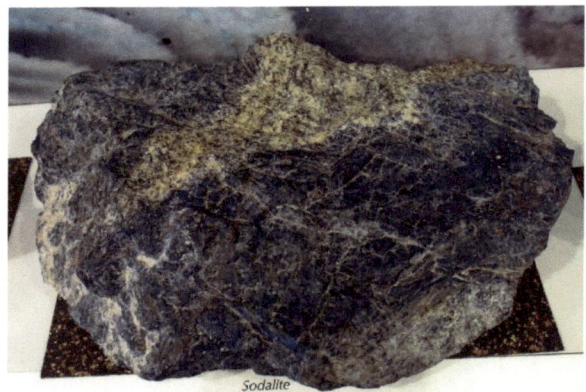
Sodalite

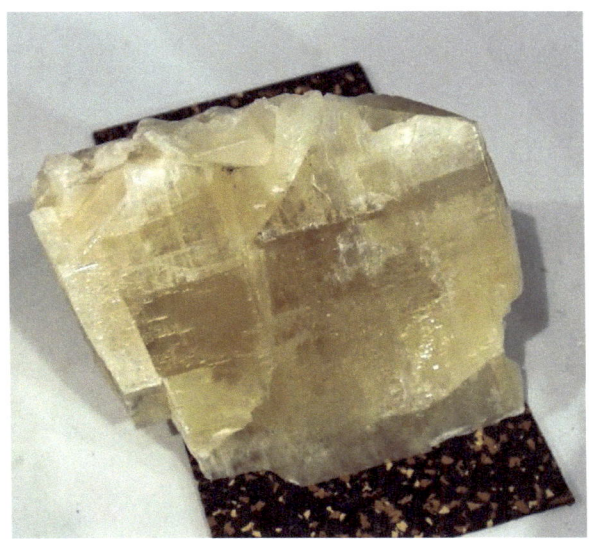

Calcite

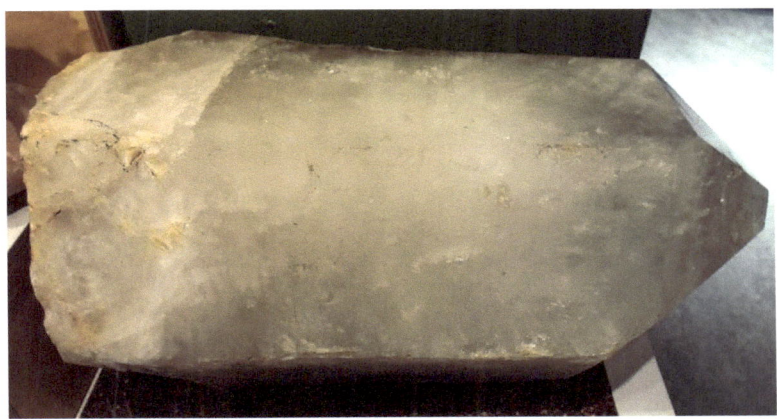

Quartz

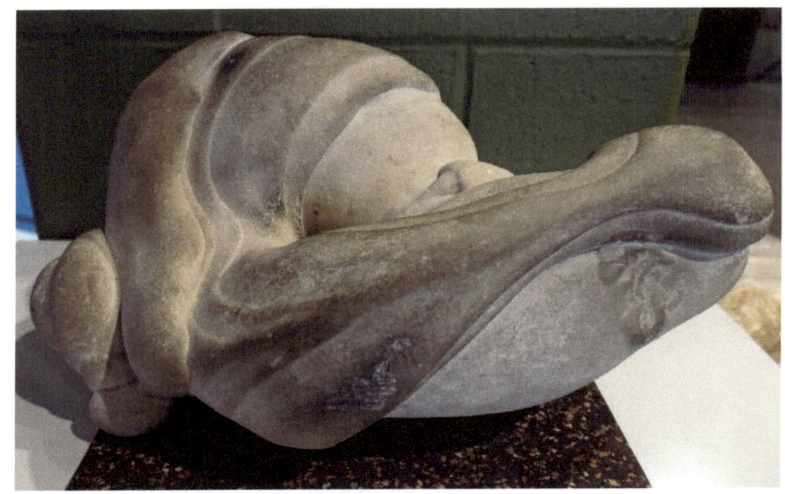
Limestone

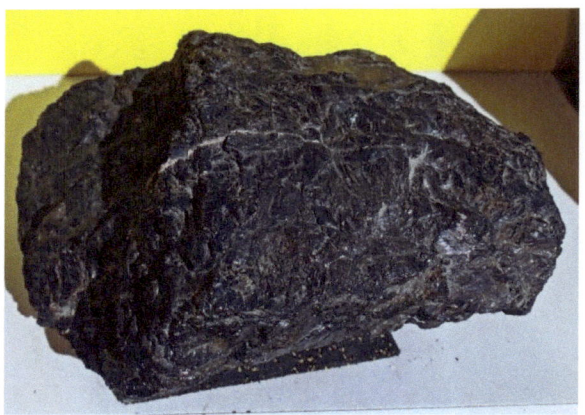
Bornite

Gold is very dense making it very heavy, but pure gold is also very soft. It doesn't rust, stretches easily into thin wire, and it can be hammered into very thin sheets. Ontario is Canada's leading producer of gold. Gold is refined from nickel-copper ore from Sudbury mines. A lot of Ontario's gold is found in volcanic and sedimentary rocks.

Gold has a rich metallic yellow colour and a brilliant lustre. In its natural form, it often appears as flakes or small irregular patches. Gold is an excellent conductor of heat and electricity.

Aluminum is very light and is the most common metal in the earth's crust. It isn't very dense and can be combined with other metals to become a light and strong alloy that is perfect for use in cars and airplanes. Aluminum is not mined anywhere in Canada. Raw material is shipped from around the world for smelting and refining in Canada.

Copper is a soft metal that is lighter than gold but heavier than aluminum. It is commonly used in coinage because it is not too heavy and not too light, and is resistant to corrosion. Ontario is Canada's second largest producer of copper. Sudbury mines have produced more than eight million tonnes of copper since the 1880s – this is enough to fill more than three hundred and fifty Olympic size swimming pools.

Nickel is a hard metal with a similar density to copper. It is used to make stainless steel and other metal alloys that are strong, can tolerate extreme temperatures, and can resist corrosion. Ontario is the leading producer of nickel in Canada, and it comes mainly from Sudbury mines.

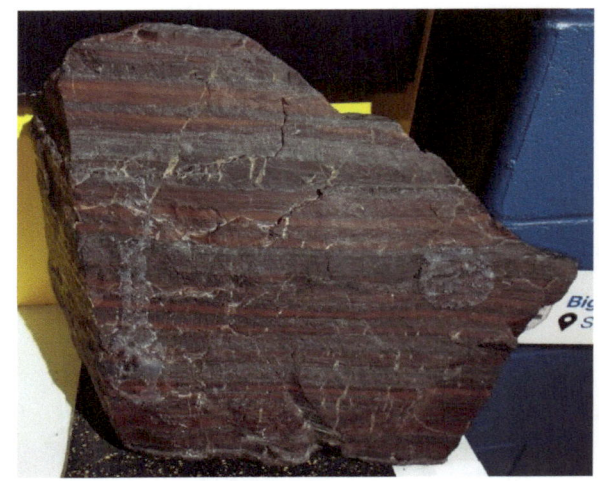
Banded Iron Formation

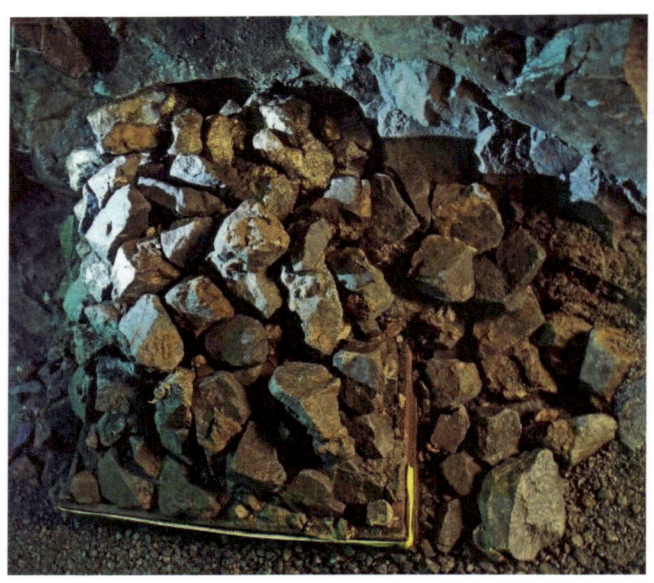

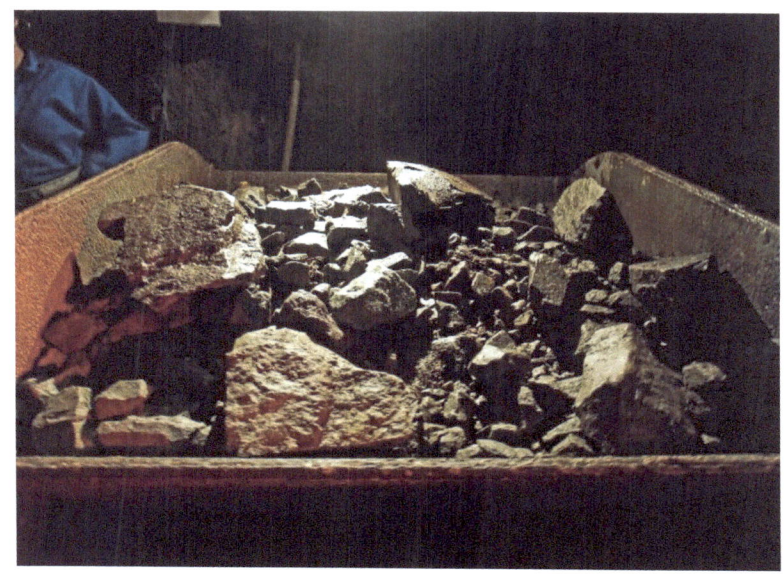

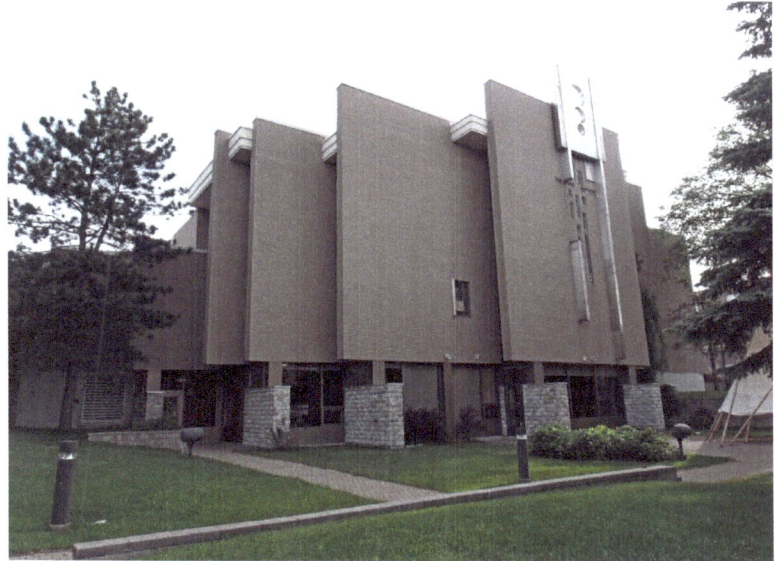

14 Beech Street - An important center of the Roman Catholic Church in northeastern Ontario, Sainte Anne des Pins was established as a mission by Jesuits in 1883. It has been housed in the present structure since 1894.

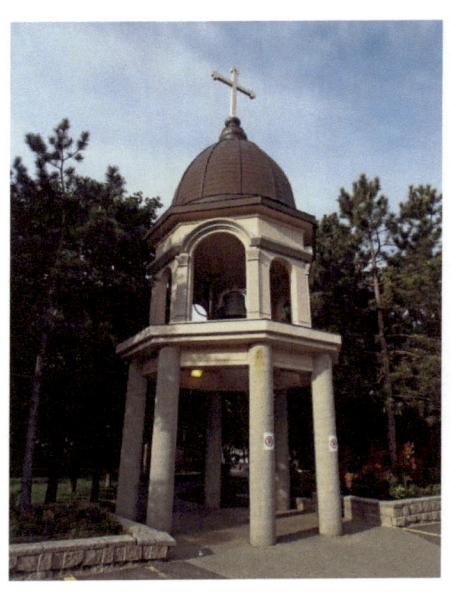

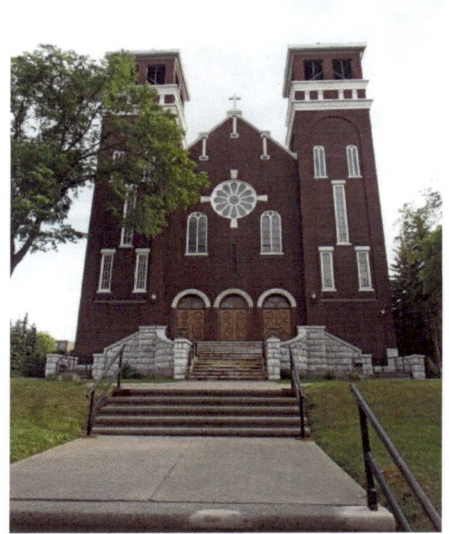

30 Beech Street – Church of Christ the King – built in 1928, gutted by fire in 1947; rebuilt and reopened in 1948.

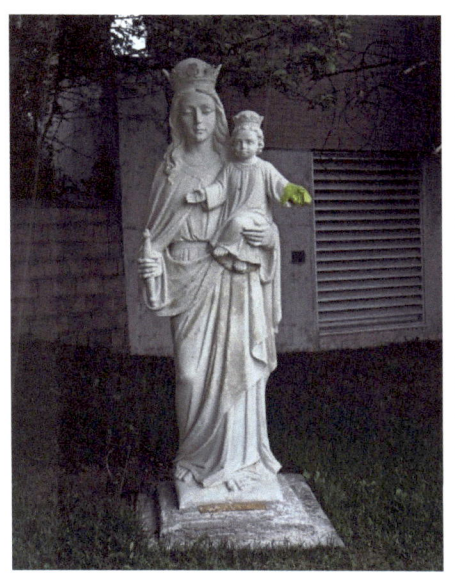 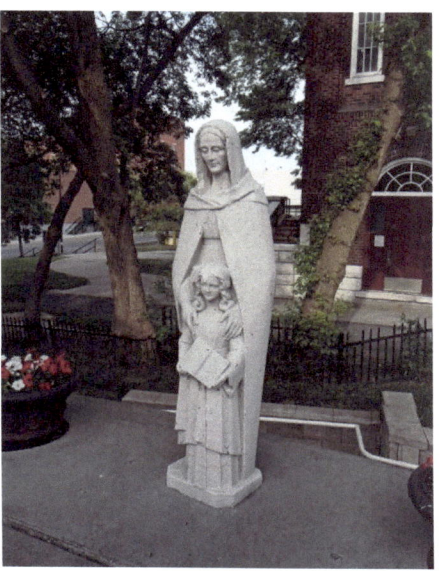

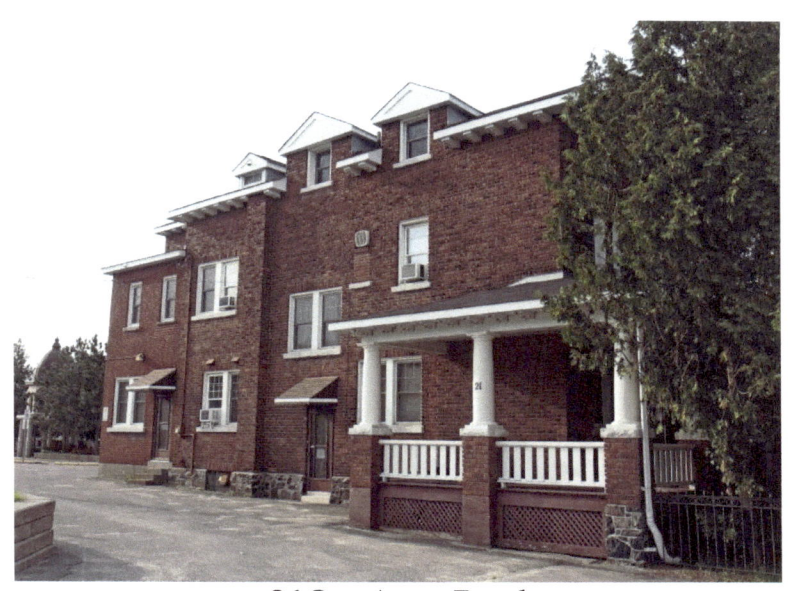

26 Ste. Anne Road

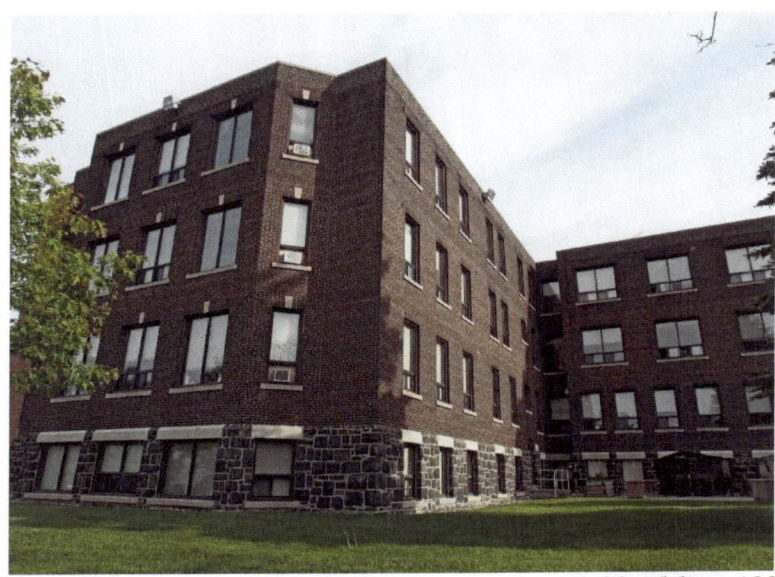

20 Ste. Anne Road – St. Joseph's Hospital - Original building 1898, Surgical Ward added 1914, 1927 modern laundry added, 1928 new heating plant with a long connecting underground tunnel. In 1975 the Hospital was closed. Partially demolished, the remaining portion is now operating as Red Oak Villa retirement home.

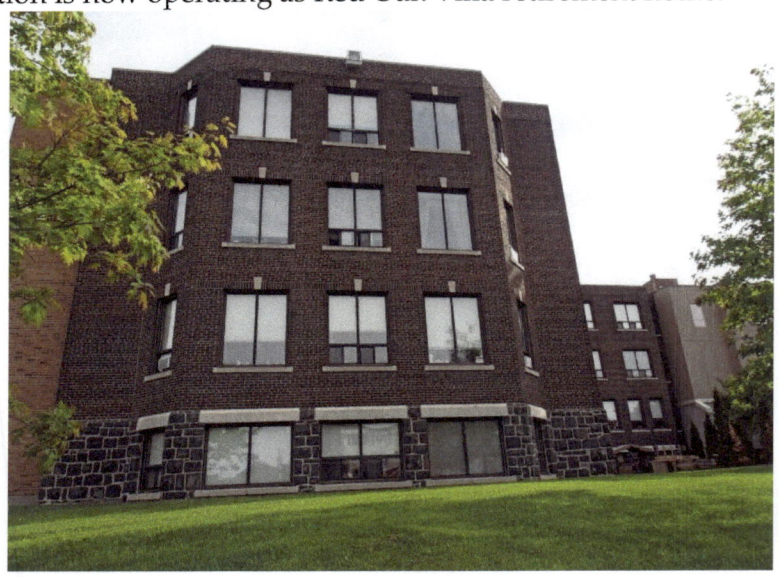

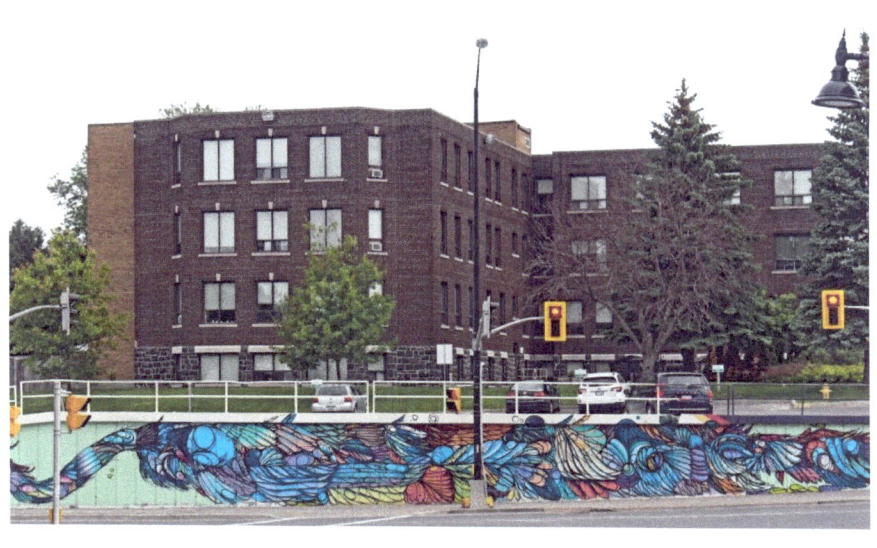

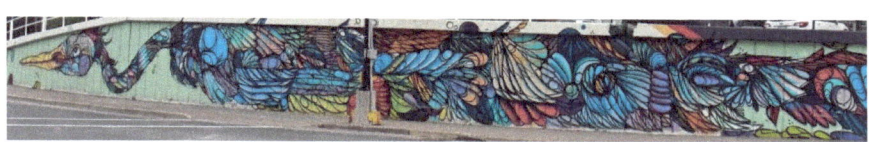

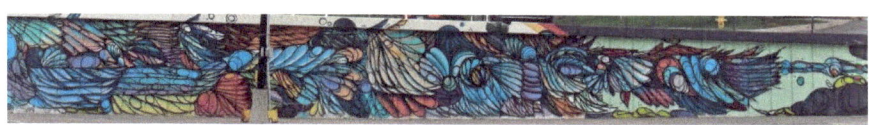

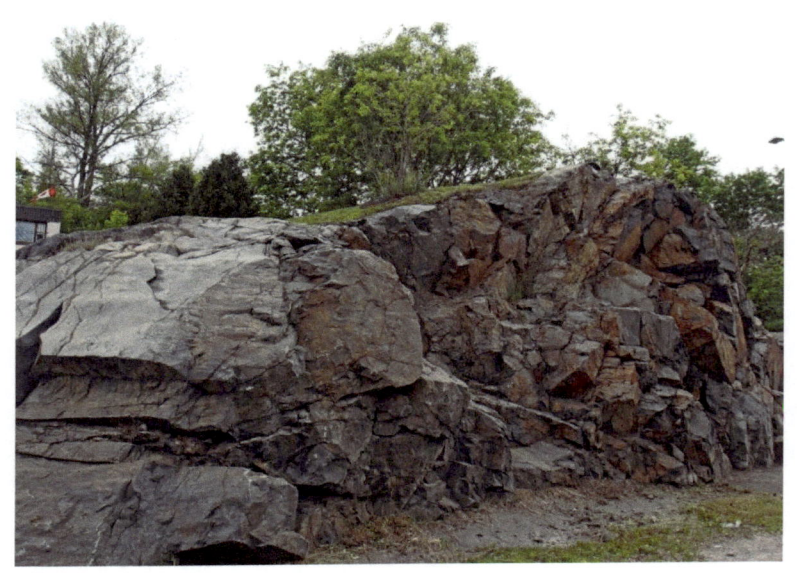

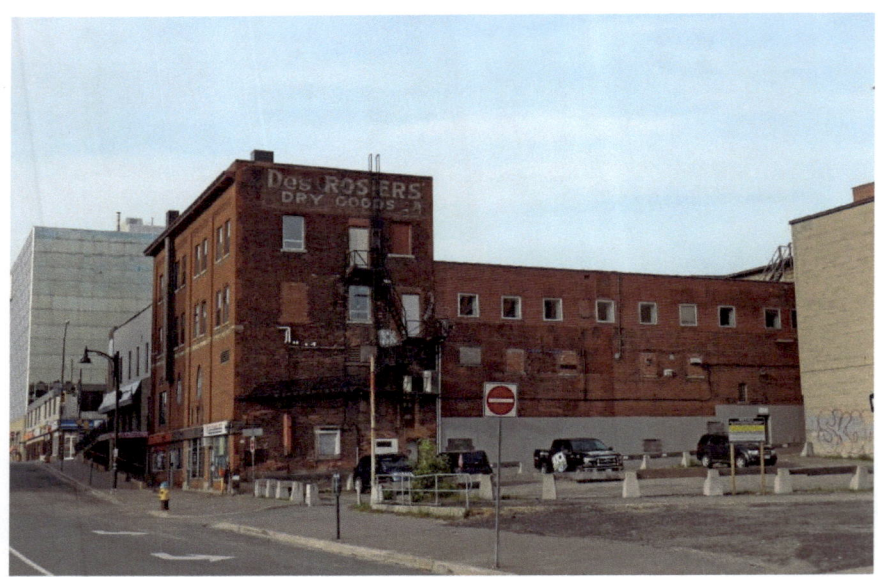

Elgin Street

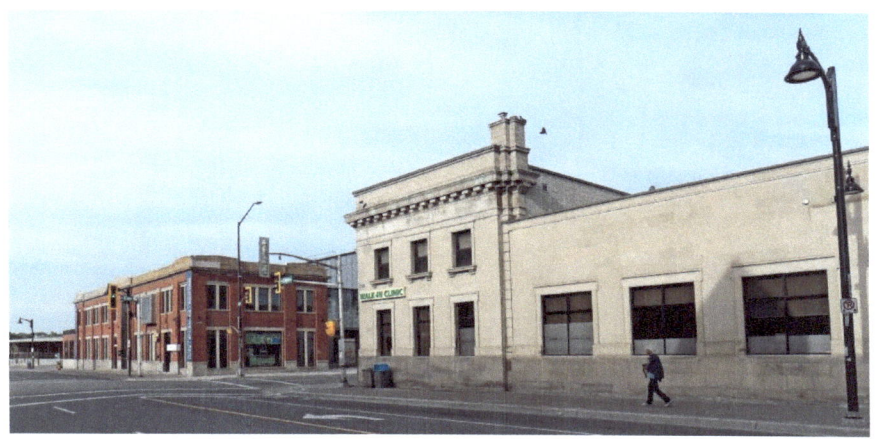
Elgin Street

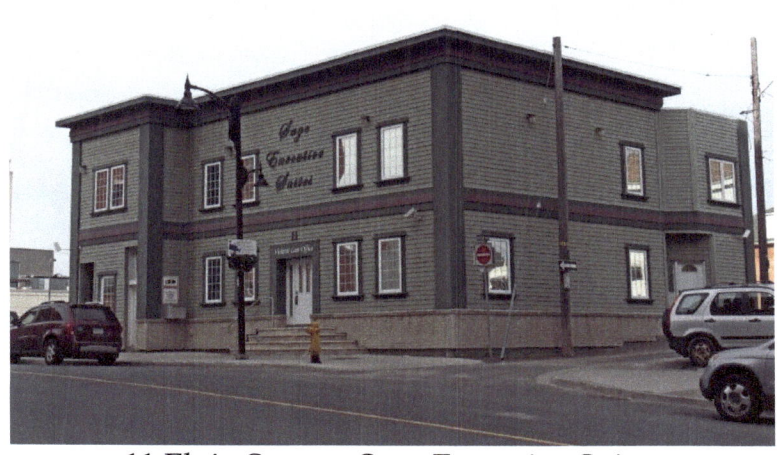
11 Elgin Street – Sage Executive Suites

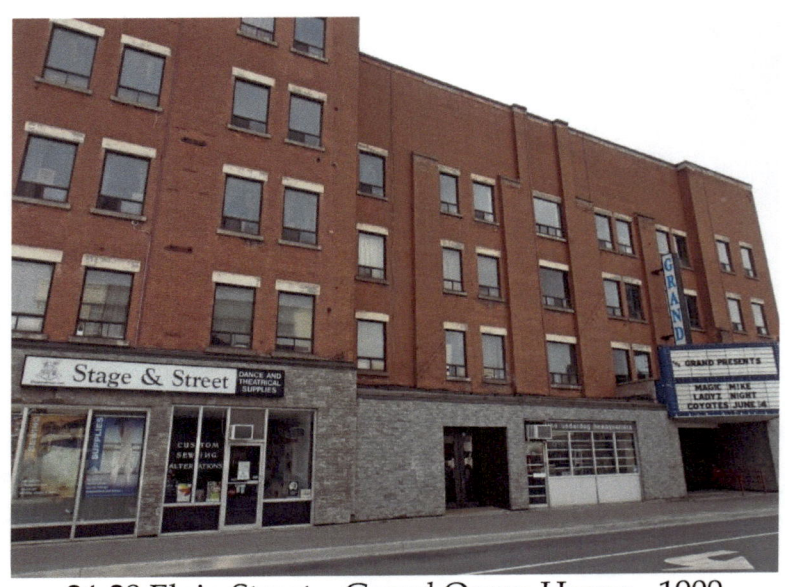

24-28 Elgin Street – Grand Opera House - 1909

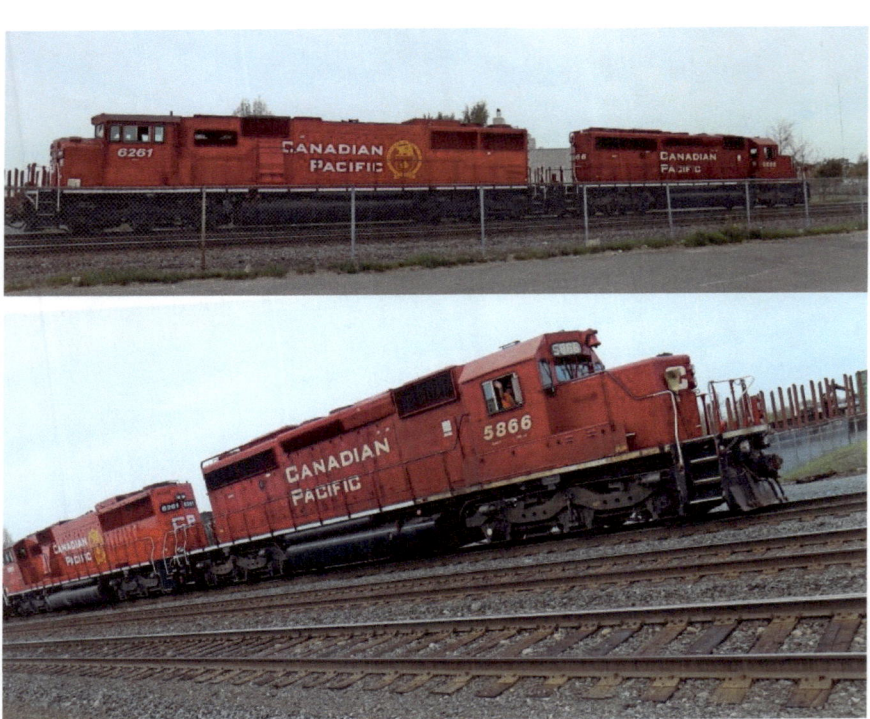

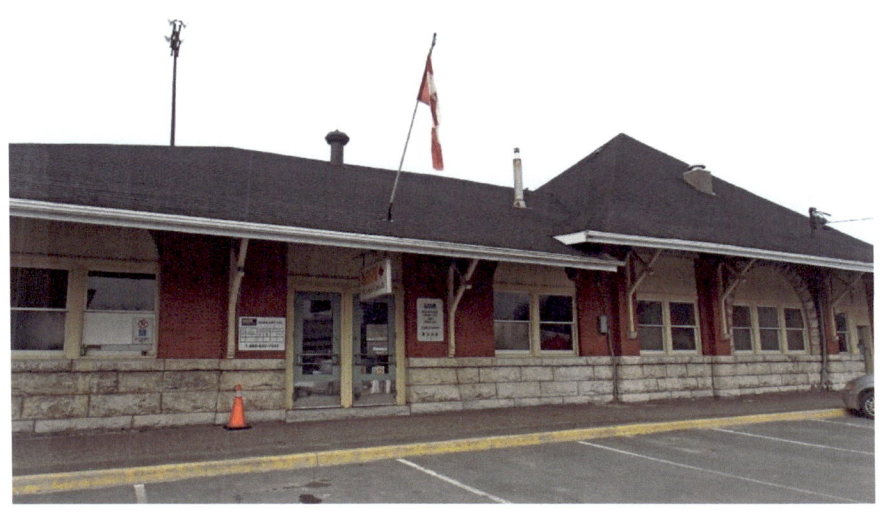

233 Elgin Street – Canadian Pacific Railway Station - 1907

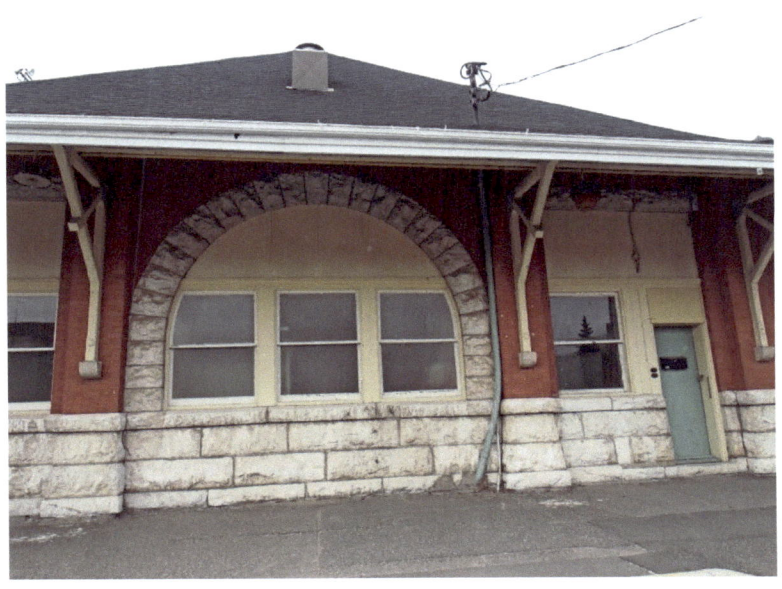

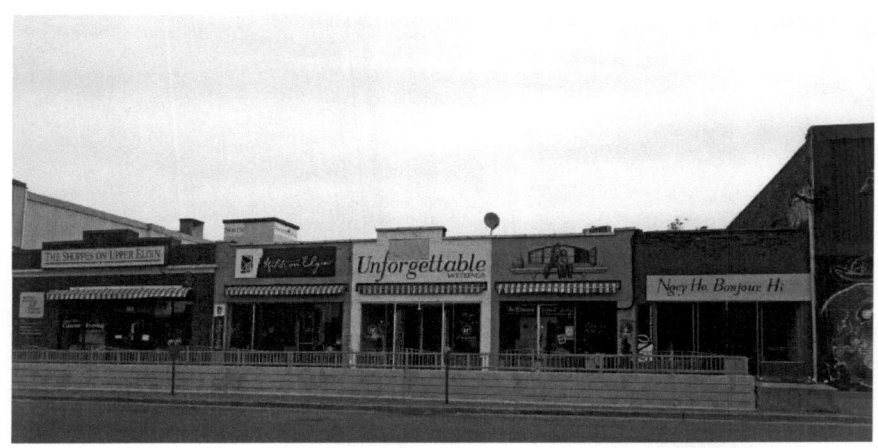

170 Elgin Street – Unforgettable Weddings

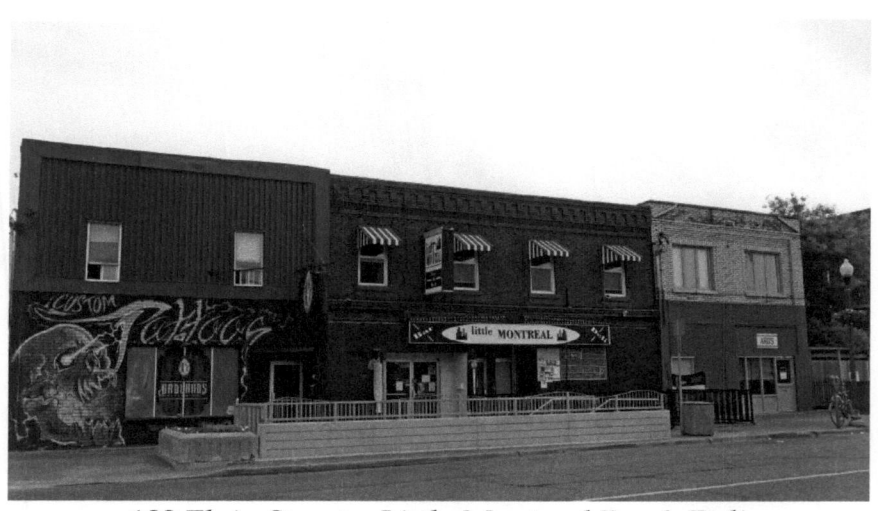

182 Elgin Street – Little Montreal Bar & Deli

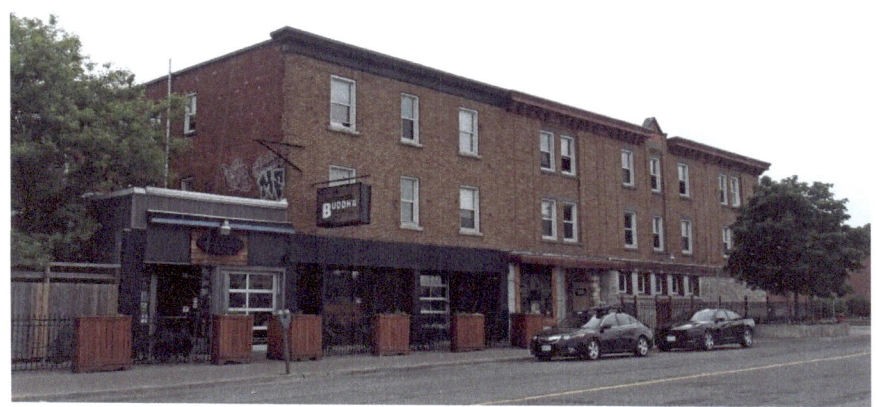

194 Elgin Street – The Laughing Buddha

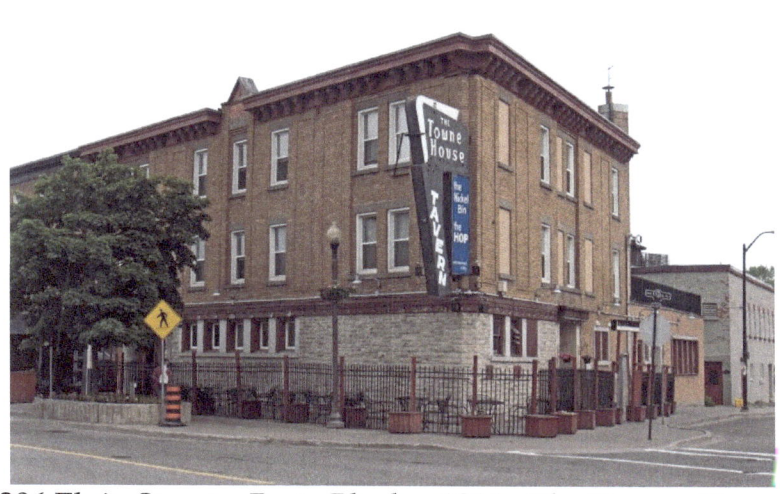

206 Elgin Street – Prete Block – 1914 - The Towne House Tavern

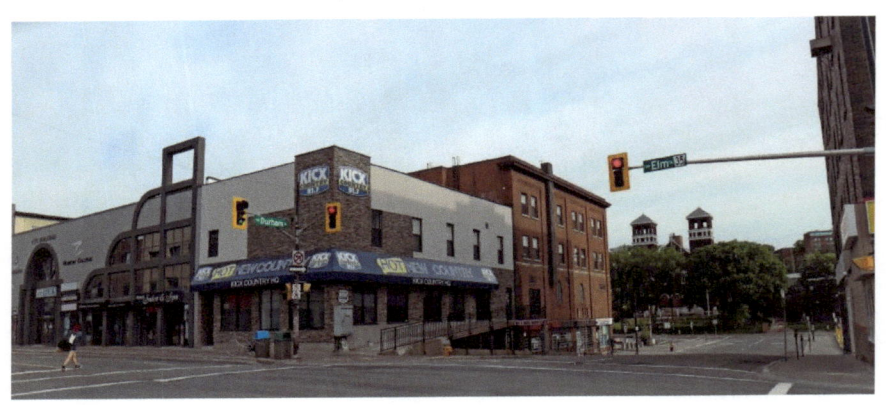

Elm Street

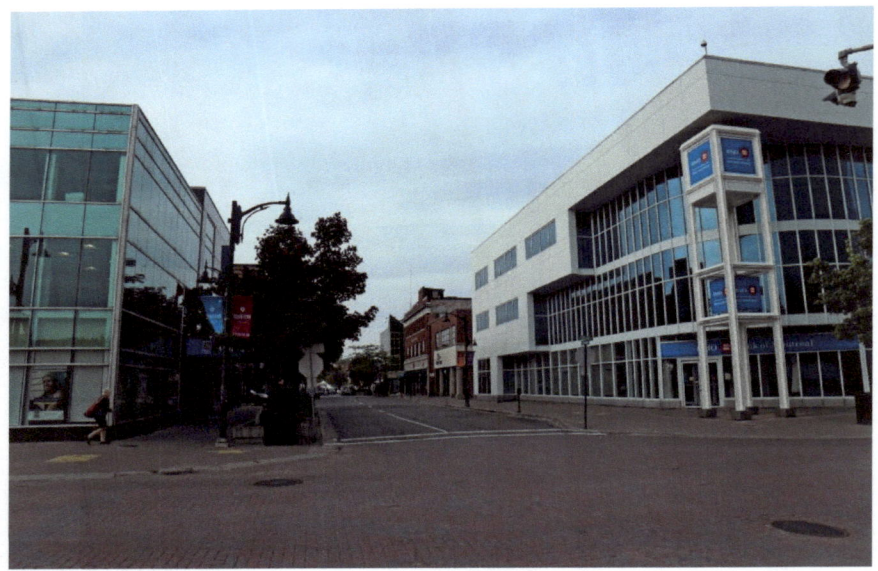

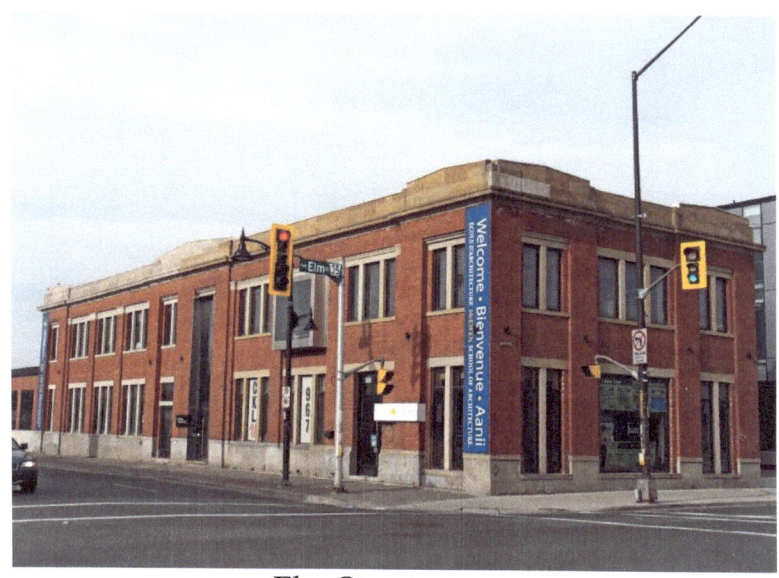

Elm Street corner

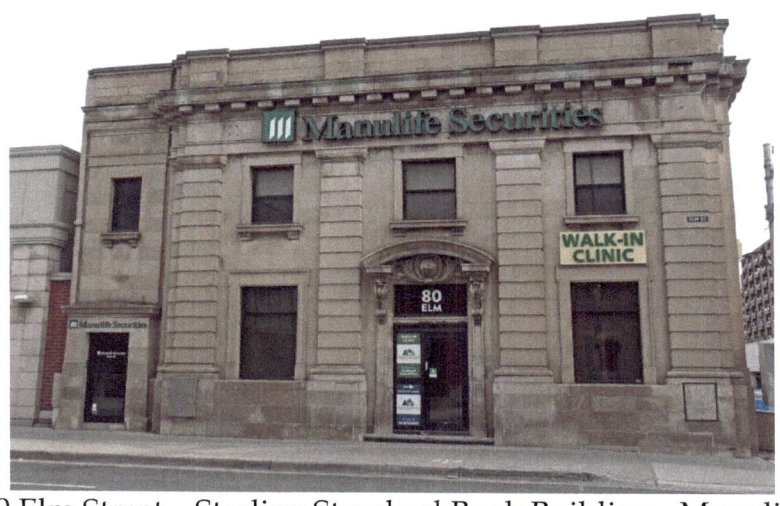

80 Elm Street – Sterling Standard Bank Building - Manulife Securities

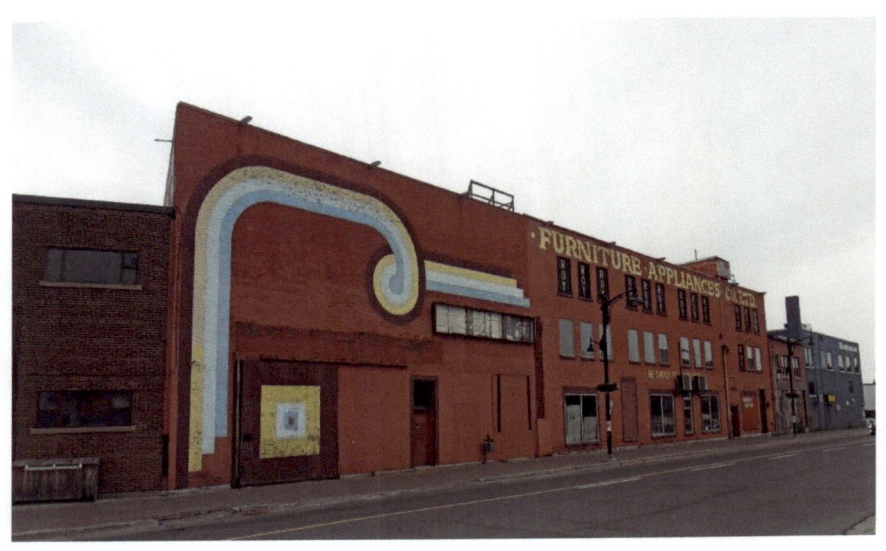

138 Elm Street – Roy Furniture and Appliances

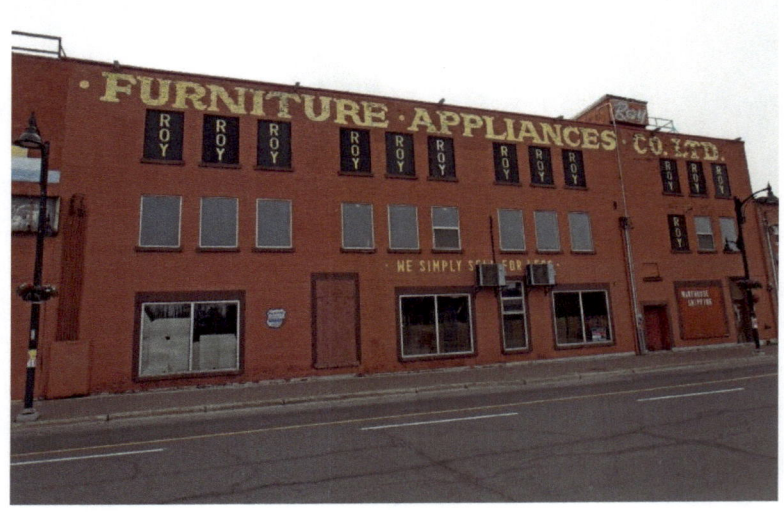

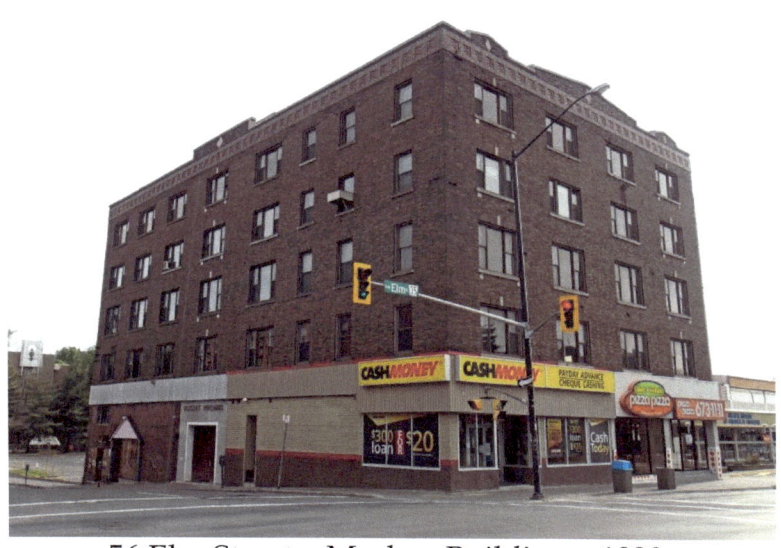

56 Elm Street – Mackey Building – 1920s

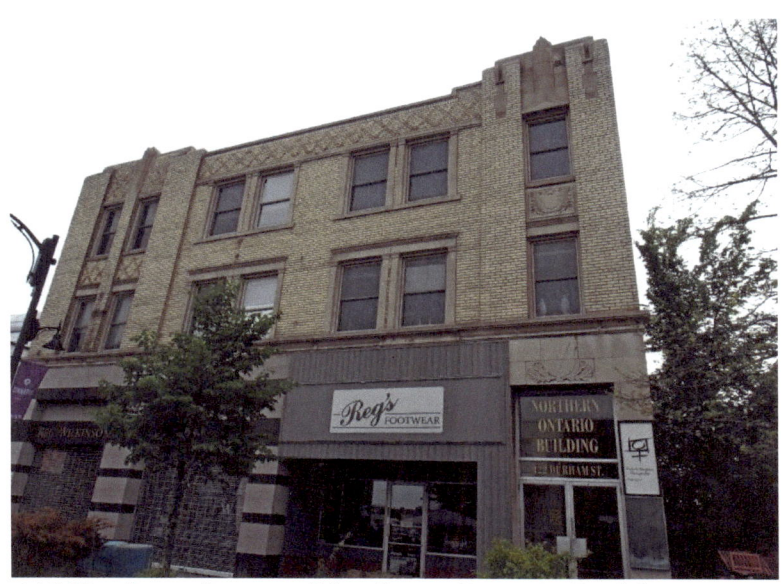

118 Durham Street – Northern Ontario Building - Reg Wilkinson Men's Fine Clothes

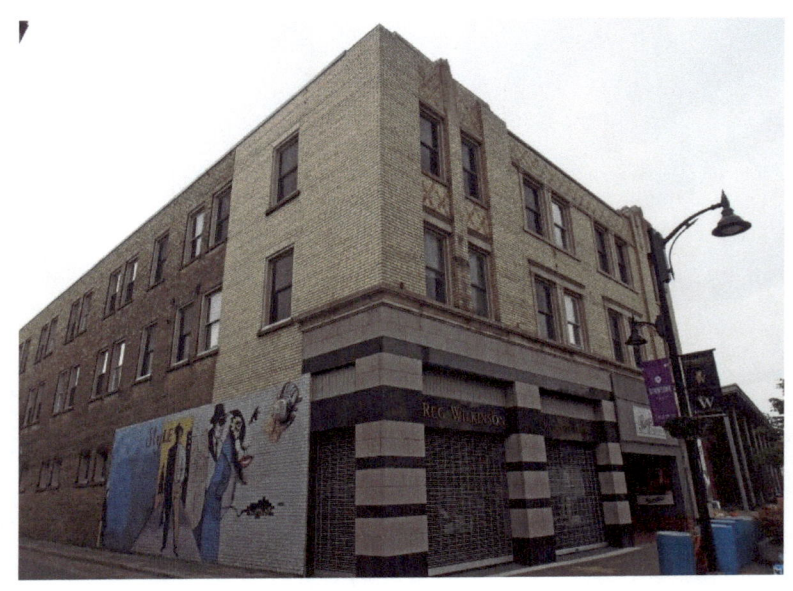

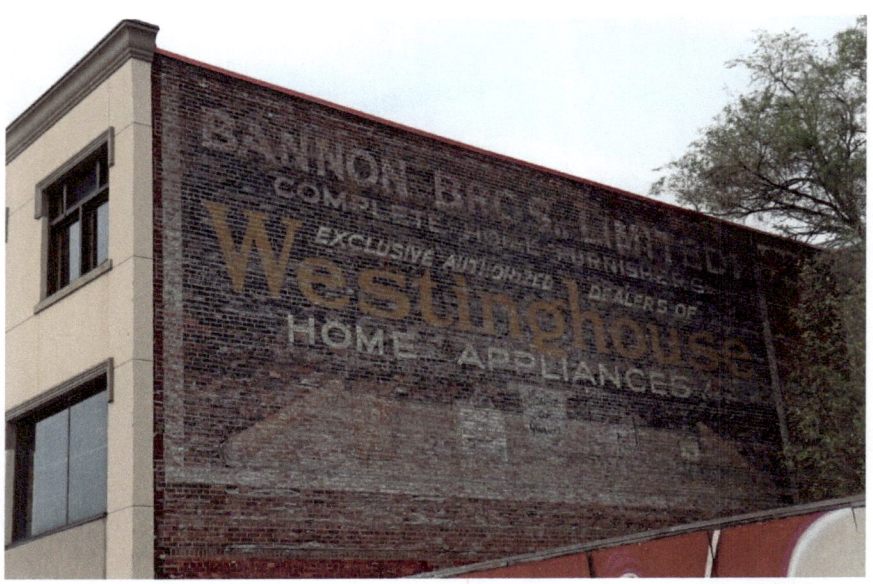

135 Durham Street – Bannon Brothers Furniture - 1923

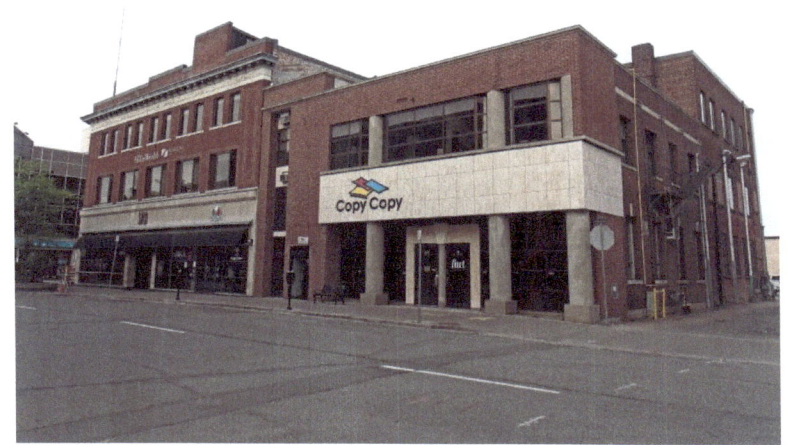

85 Durham Street

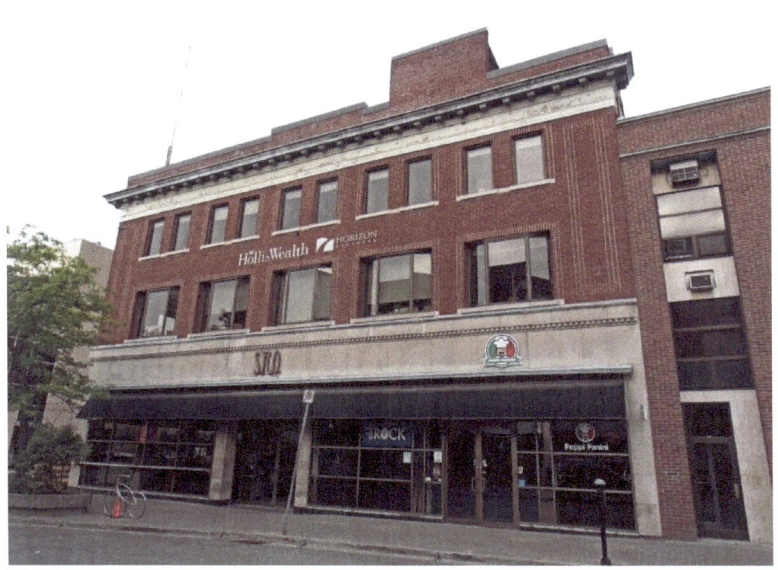

93 Durham Street – Stafford Block – originally built as a department store in 1916

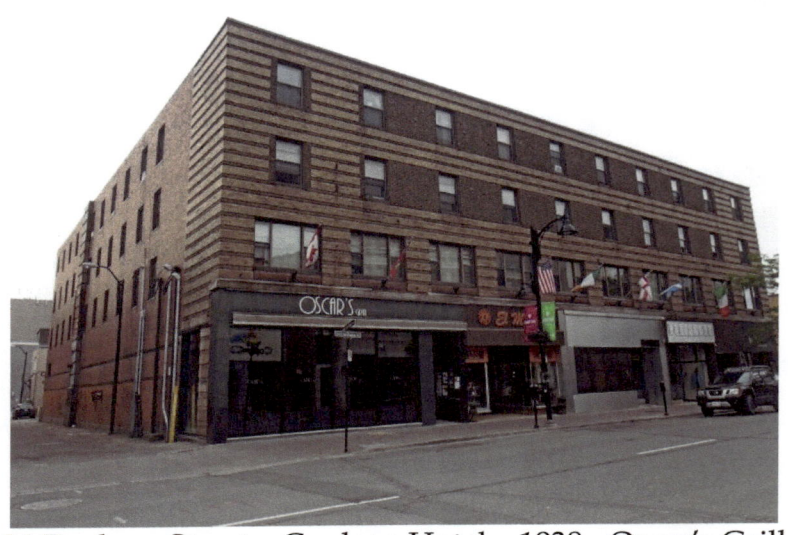

86 Durham Street – Coulson Hotel – 1938 - Oscar's Grill

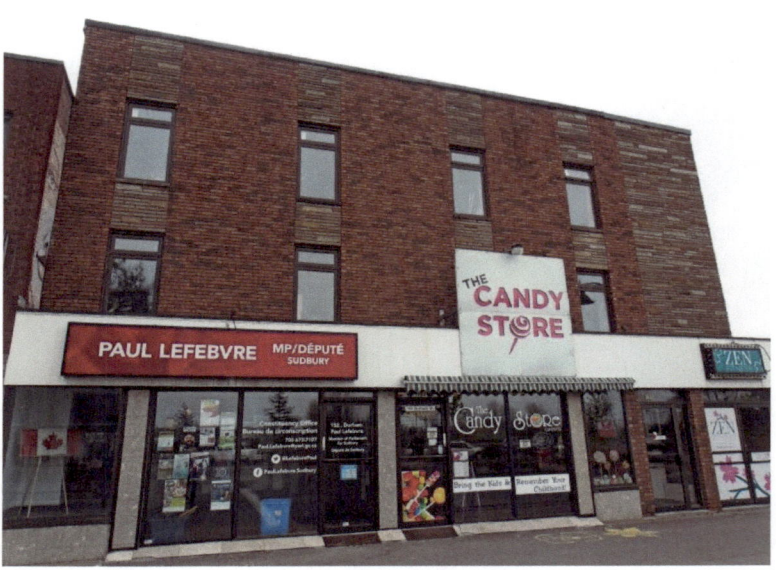

154 Durham Street – The Candy Store

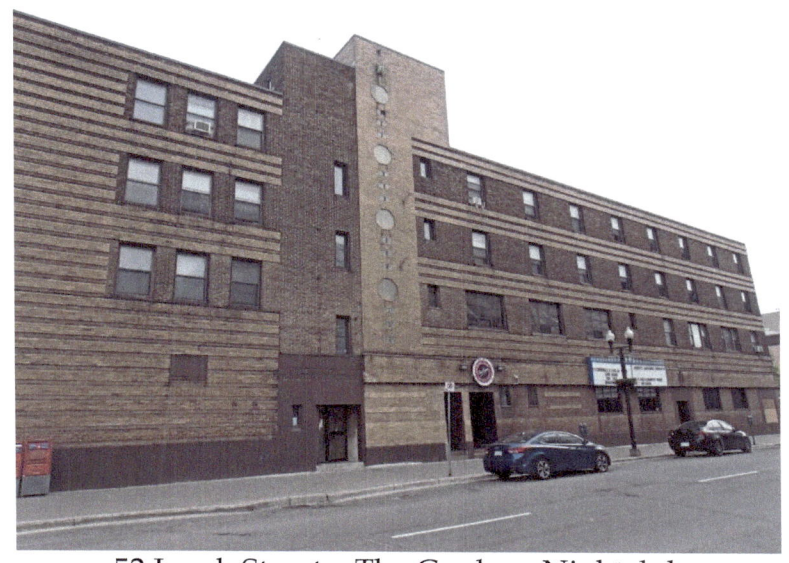

52 Larch Street – The Coulson Nightclub

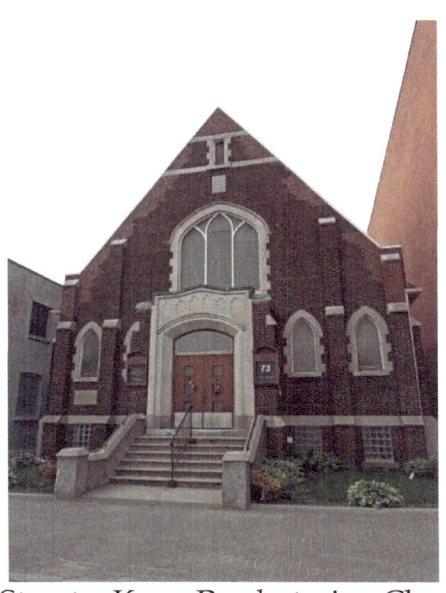

73 Larch Street – Knox Presbyterian Church - 1927

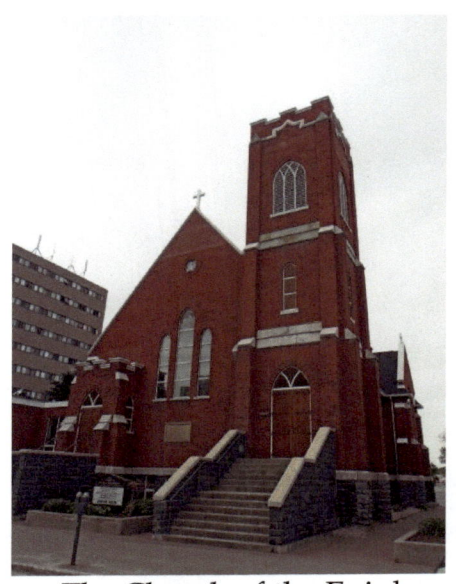

85 Larch Street – The Church of the Epiphany (Anglican) - 1913

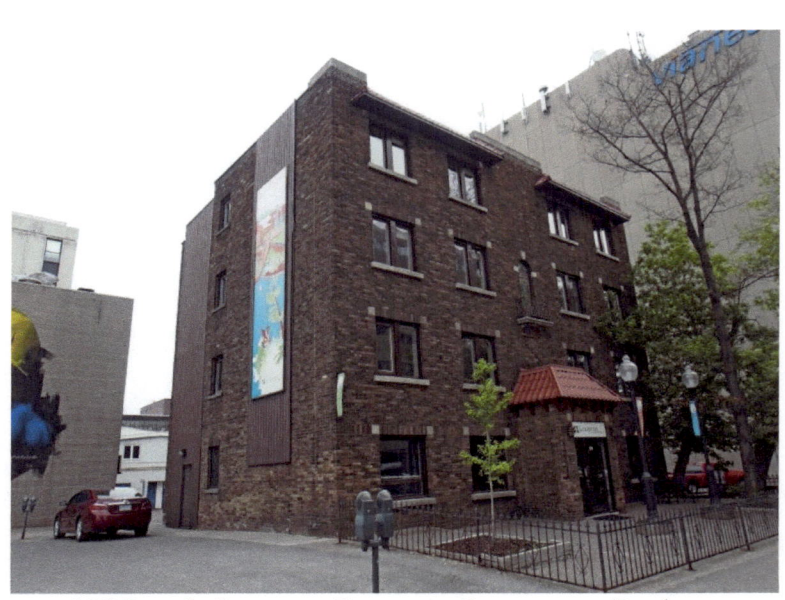

120 Larch Street – Cougeon Insurance Brokers

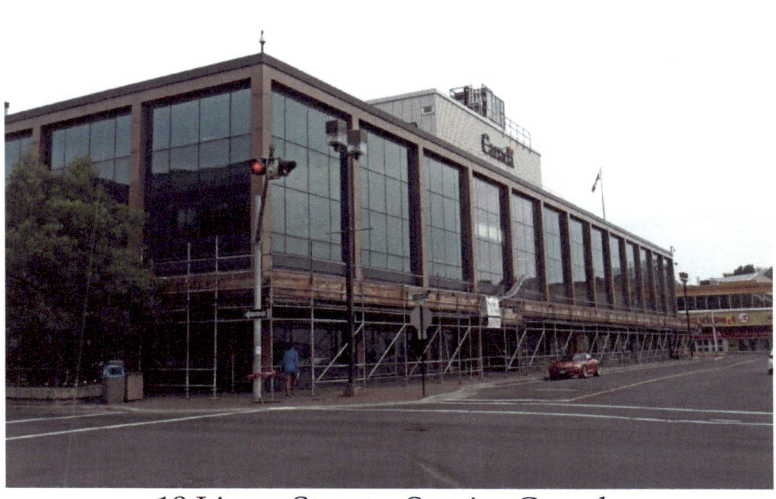

96 Larch Street – Tandoori Tastes Restaurant

19 Lisgar Street – Service Canada

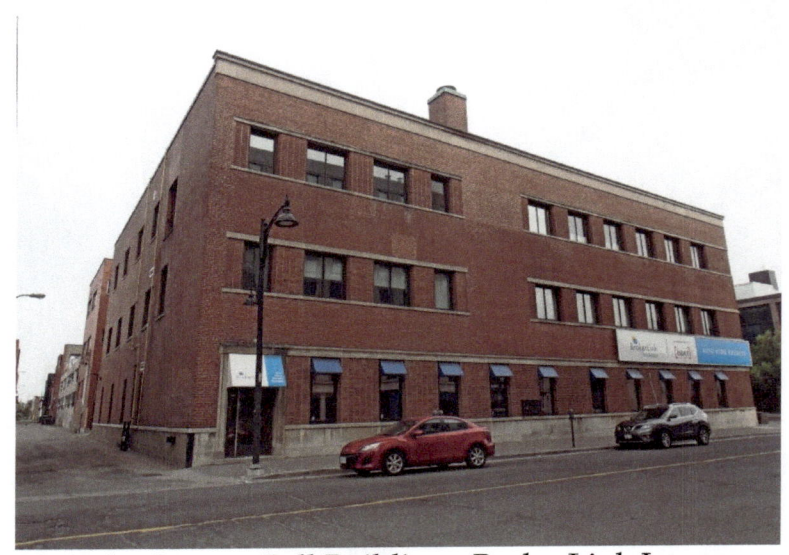
93 Cedar Street – Bell Building - BrokerLink Insurance

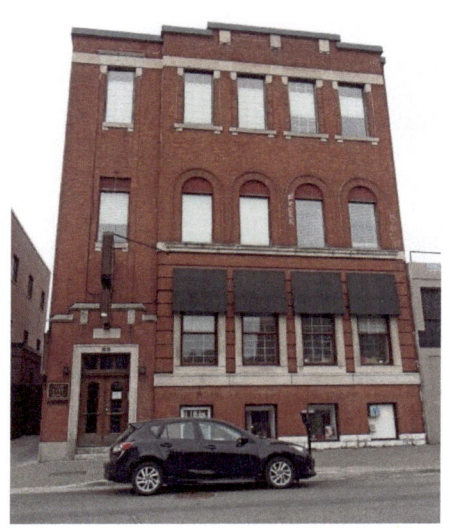
88 Cedar Street – Old City Hall

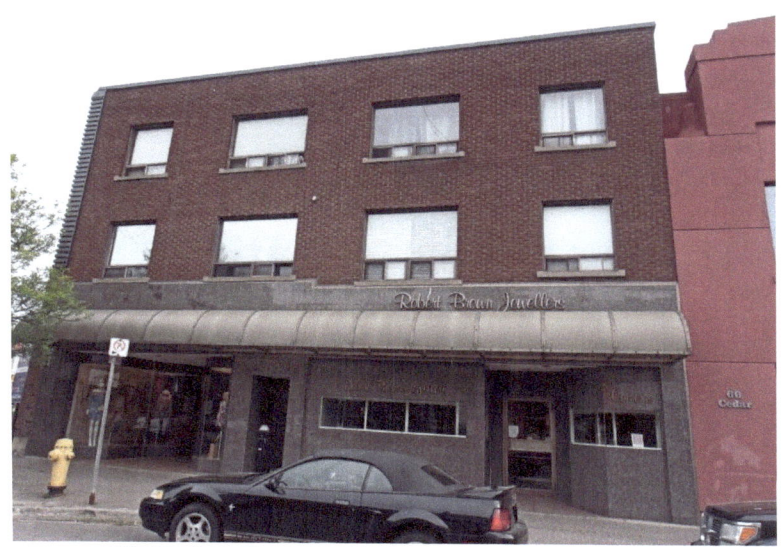

62 Cedar Street – Robert Brown Jewellers

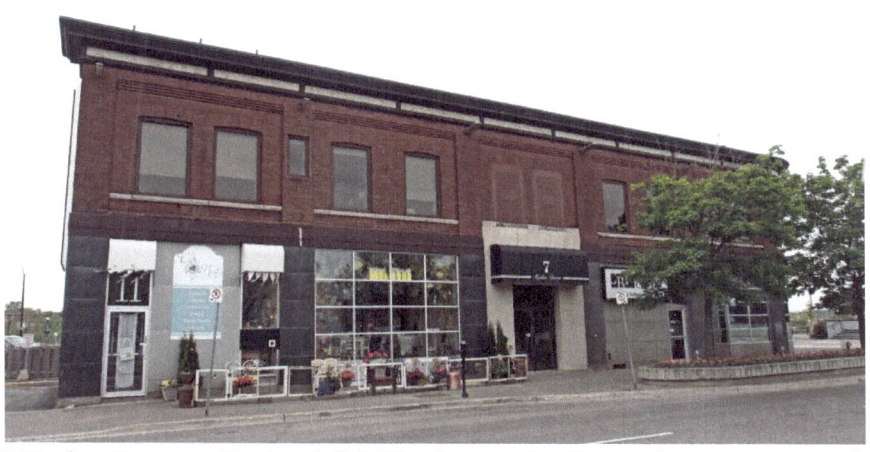

7 Cedar Street - Rothschild Block was built on the property of Daniel Rothschild, one of Sudbury's first prosperous Jewish settlers and the father of National Hockey League player Samuel Rothschild.

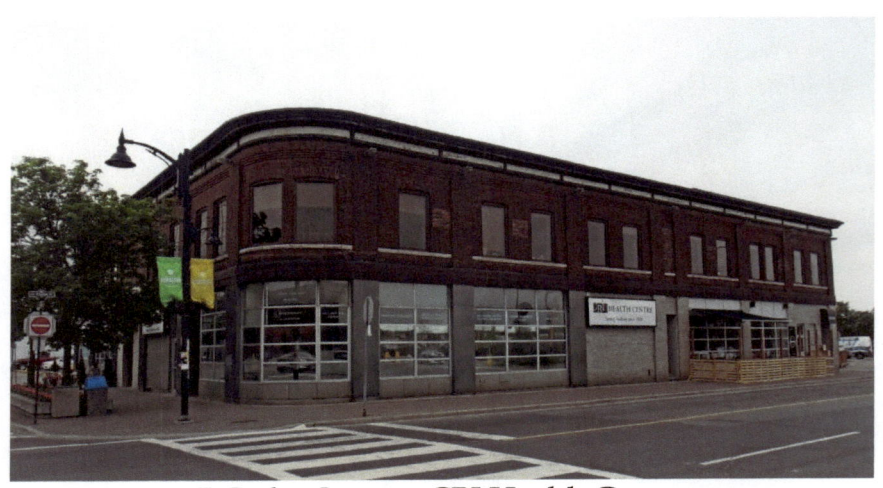

5 Cedar Street – CBI Health Group

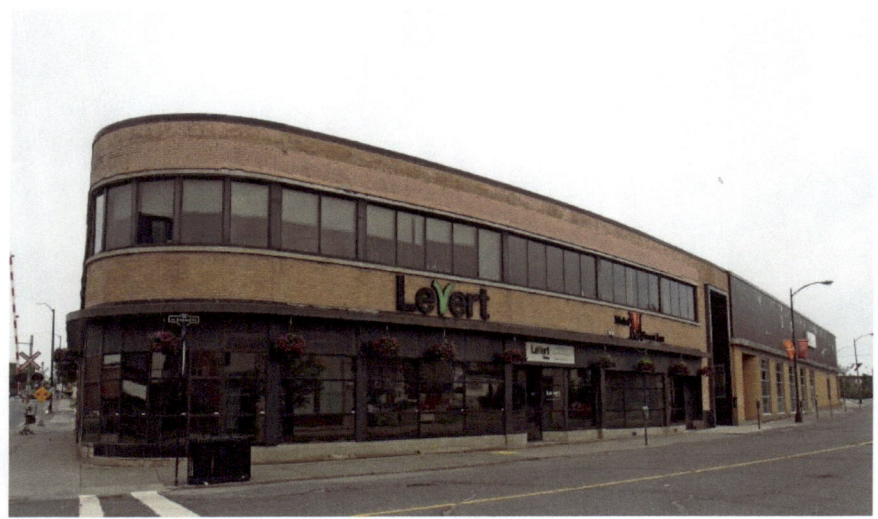

17 Frood Road – Levert

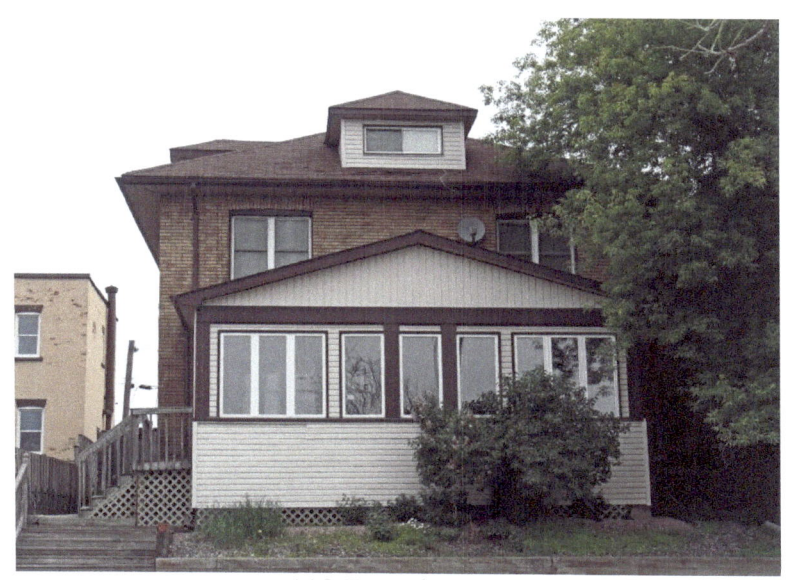

112 Frood Road

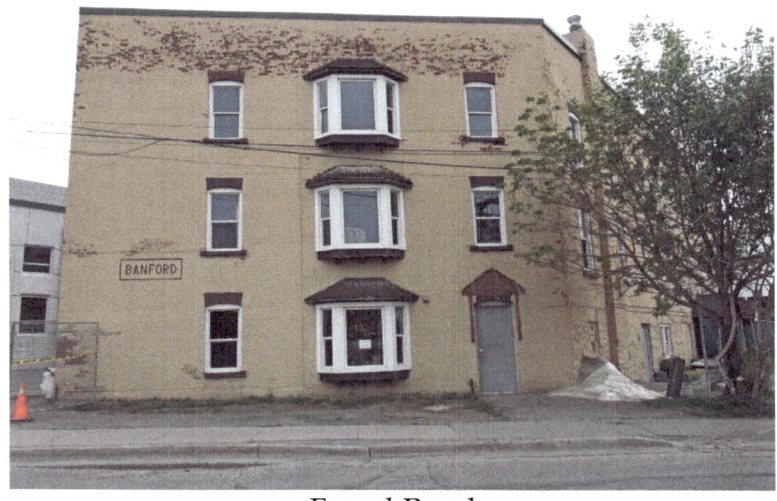

Frood Road

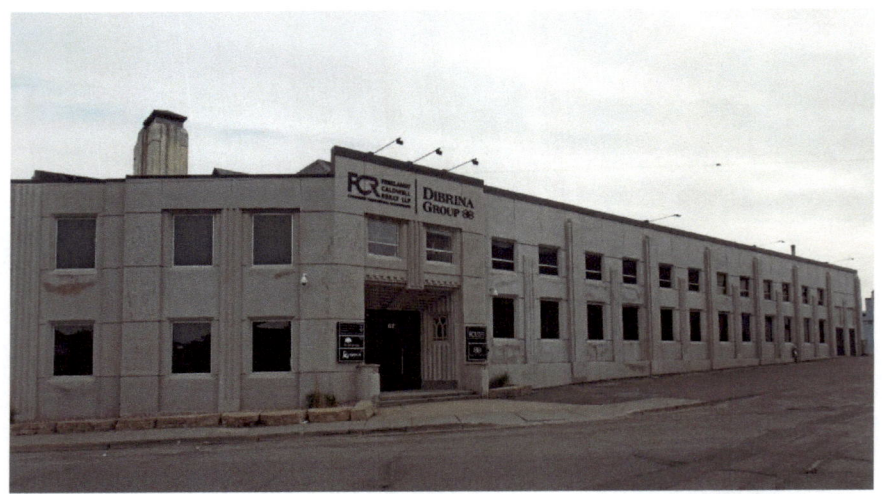

62 Frood Road – Inco Club – 1938 - Freelandt Caldwell Reilly Accountants – DiBrina Group

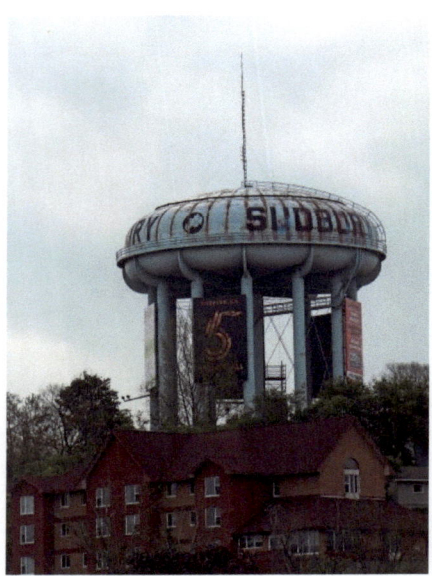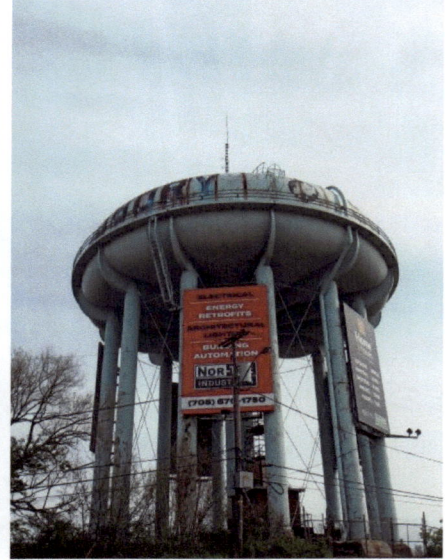

The Pearl Street Water Tower was designed and built by Horton Steel Works of Fort Erie

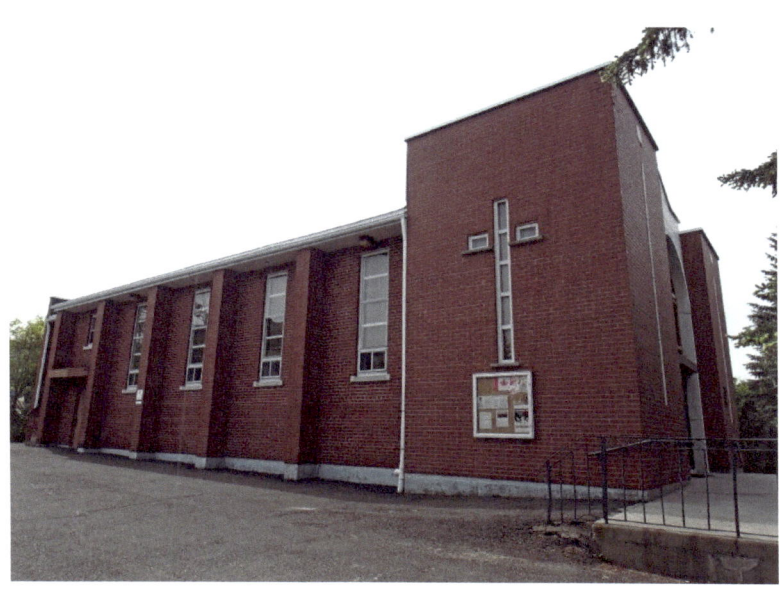

210 Paris Street – St. Casimir's Roman Catholic Church – 1956

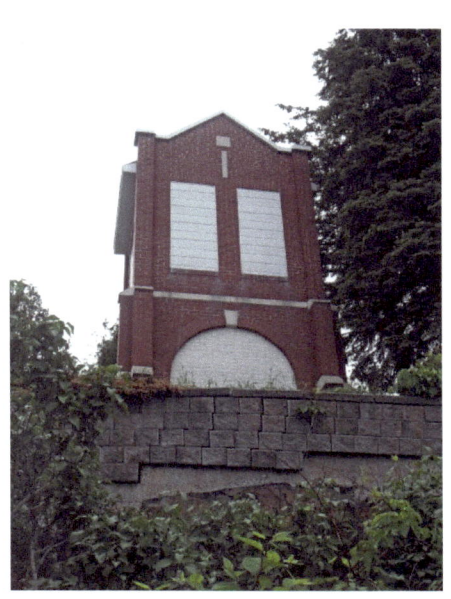
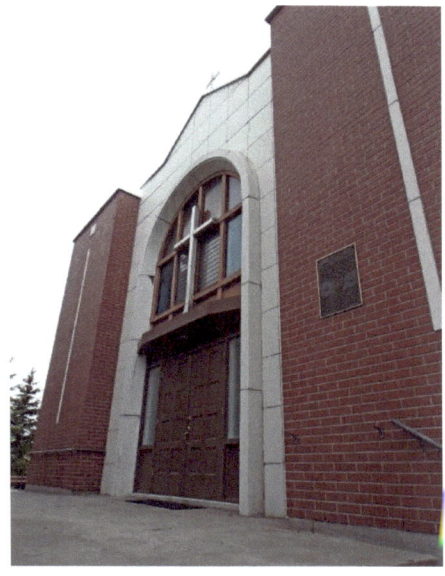

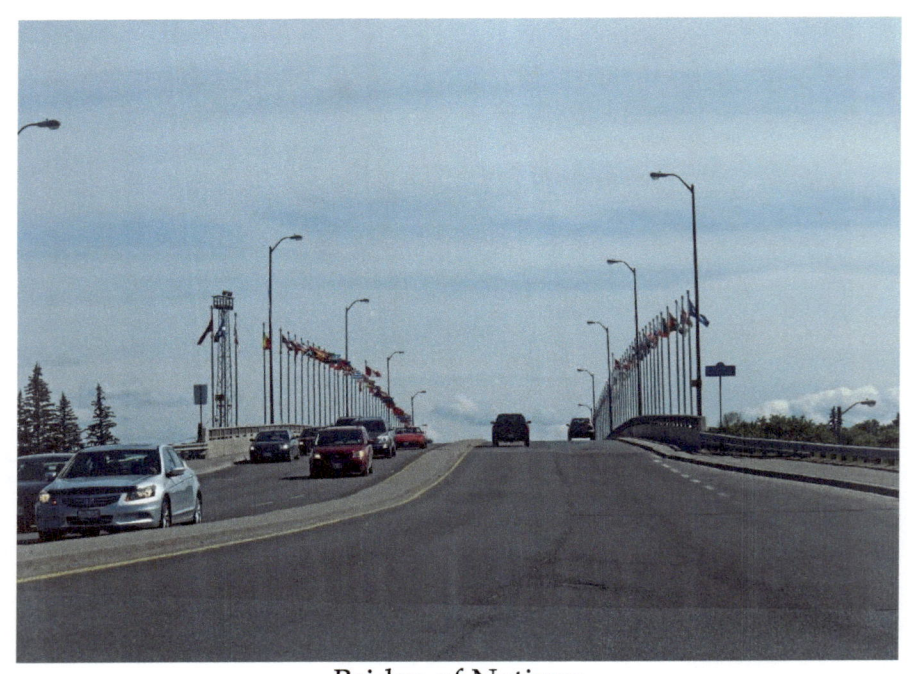
Bridge of Nations

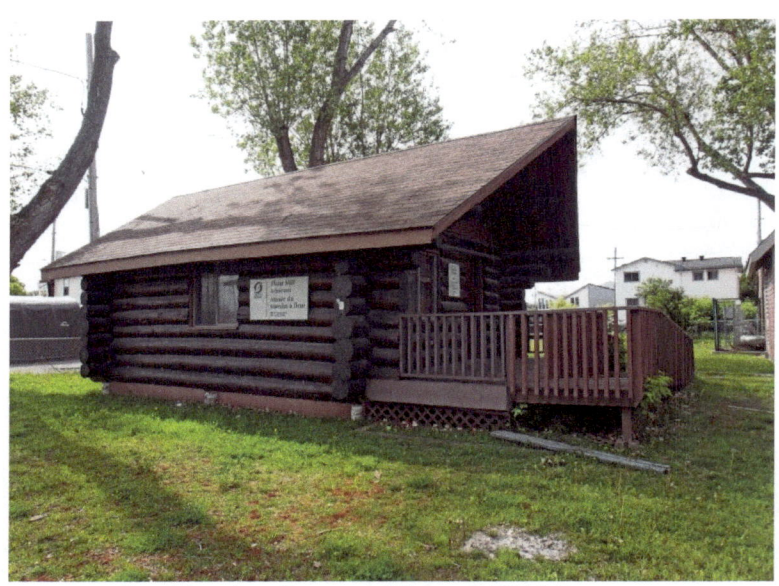
St. Charles Street - Flour Mill Museum

The Flour Mill Museum used to be located on Notre-Dame Avenue beside the Flour Mill Silos. In the 1980s it was moved to its present location on St. Charles Street. The historic building was originally the home of François Varieur, the foreman of an early lumber mill in the Sudbury area. It was later acquired by the Manitoba and Ontario Flour Mill Company, to serve as the home of the community's flour mill foreman.

The museum was opened in 1974, and is devoted to the life and history of the Franco-Ontarian community in the Flour Mill area.

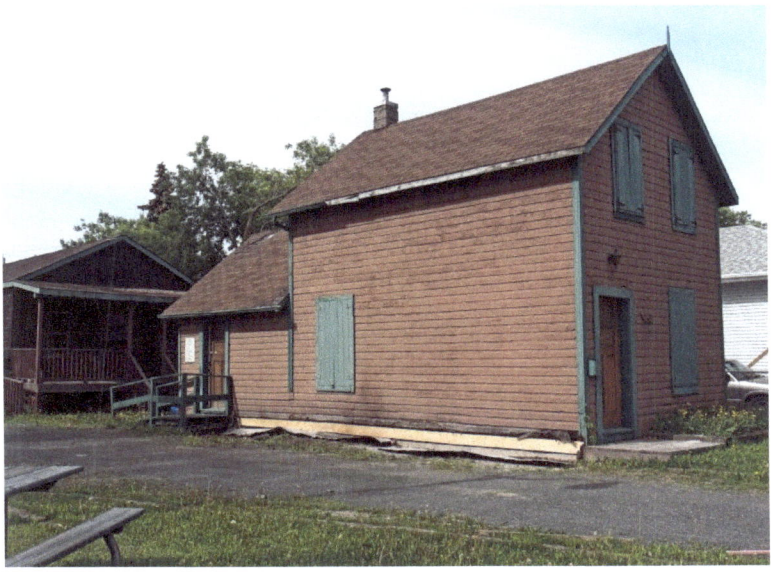

1903 clapboard house

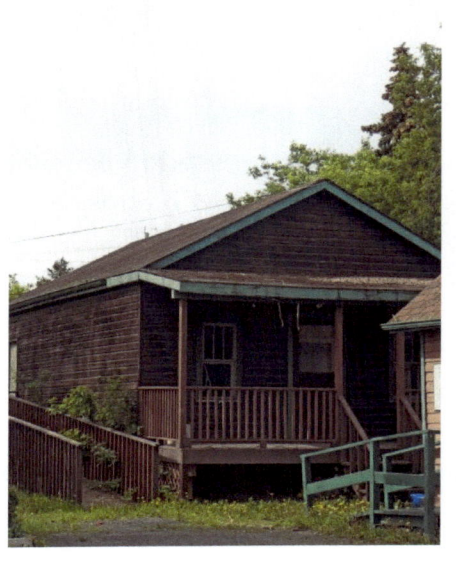

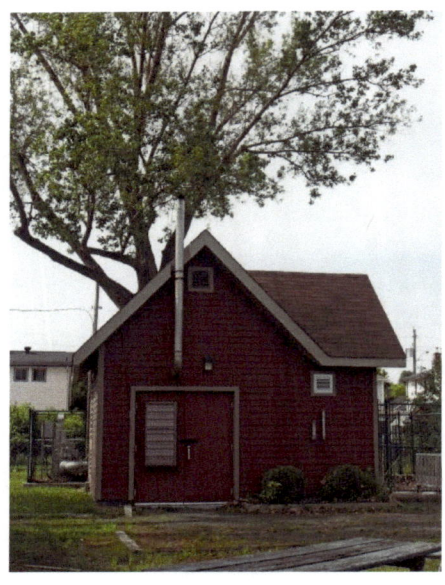

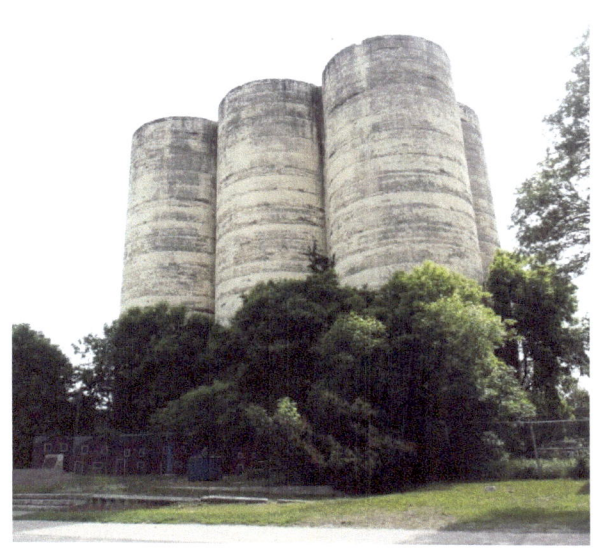

Notre Dame Avenue - Flour Mill Silos

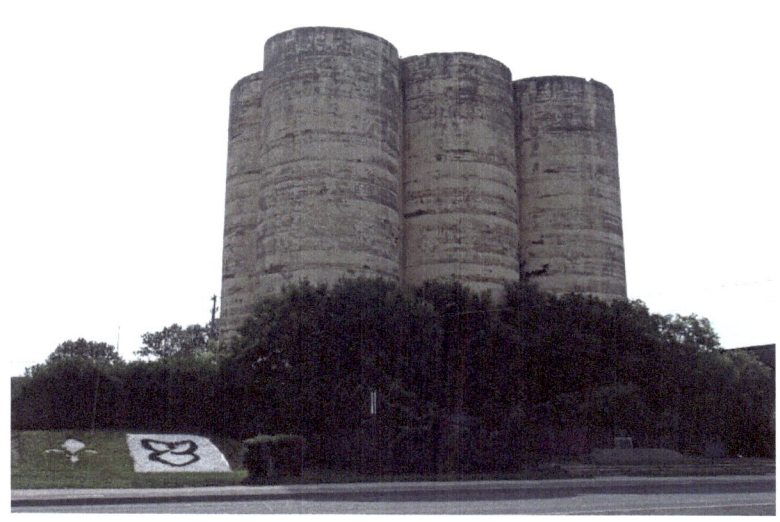

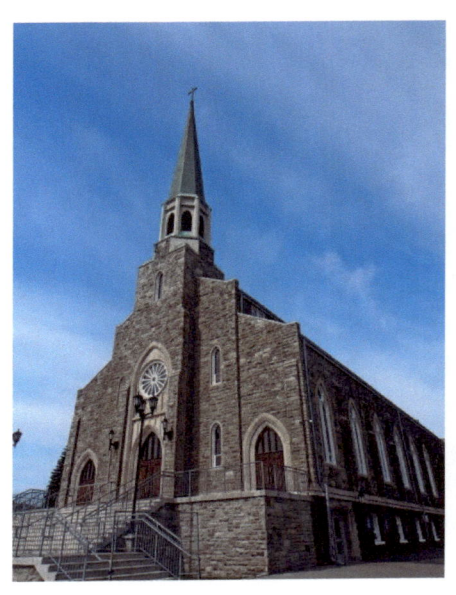

Church on Notre Dame Avenue

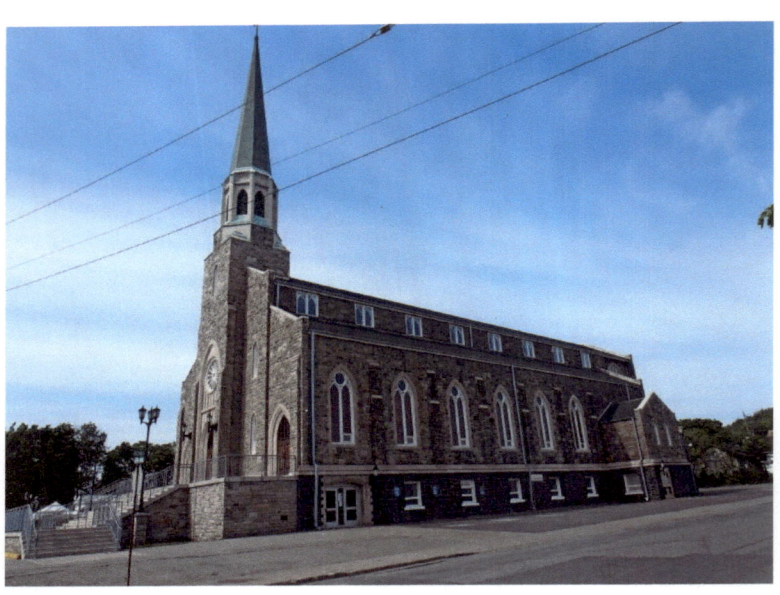

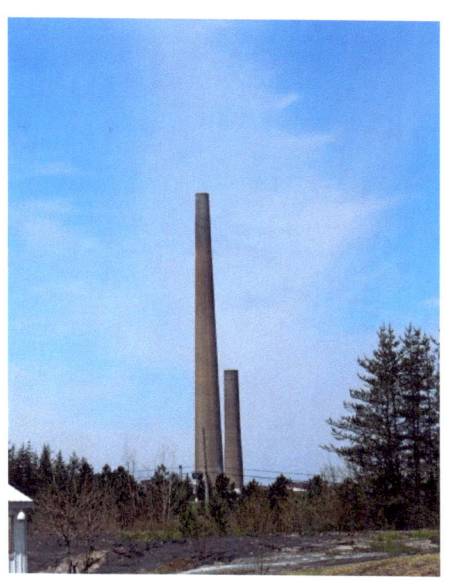

18 Rink Street – Inco Super stack

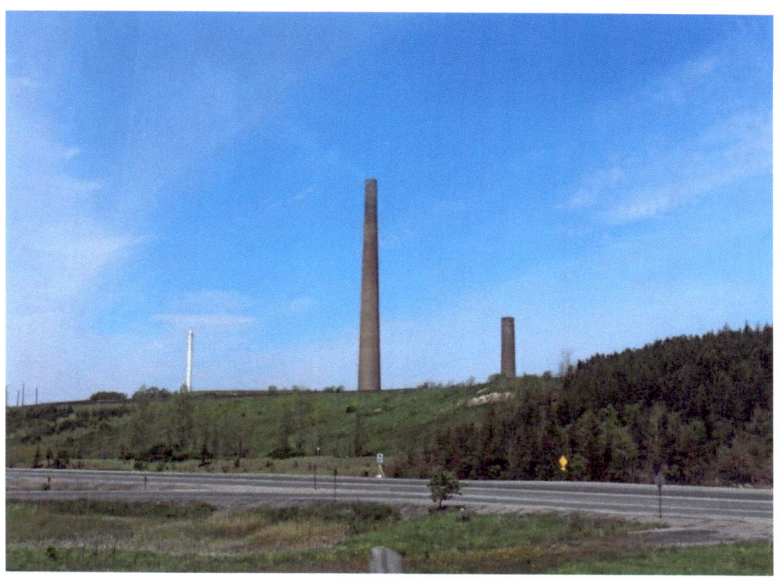

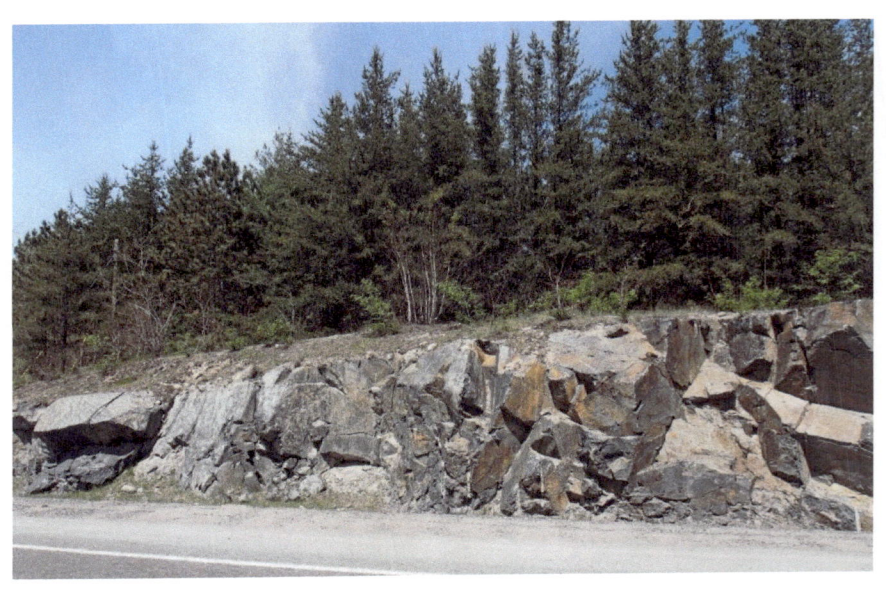

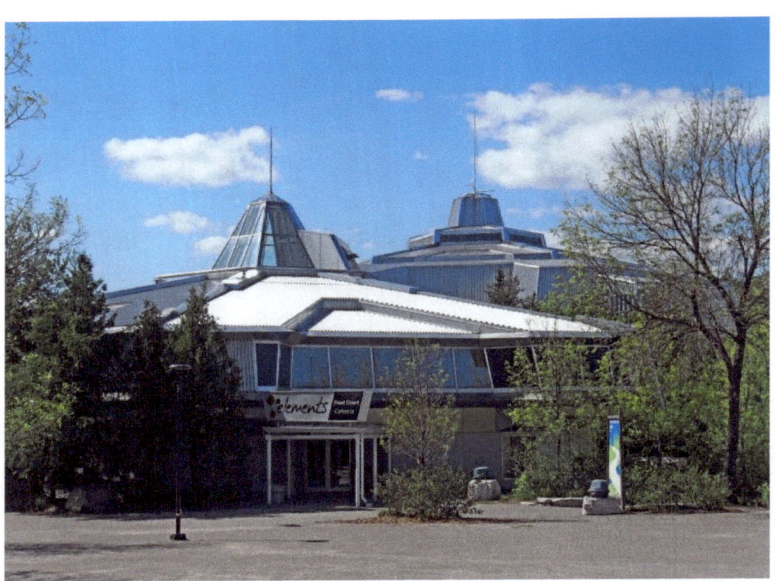

100 Ramsey Lake Rd - Science North

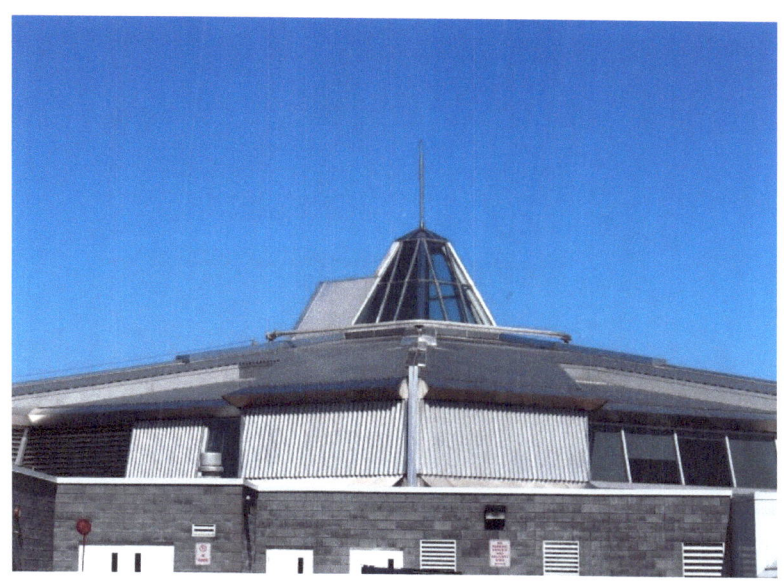

Science North

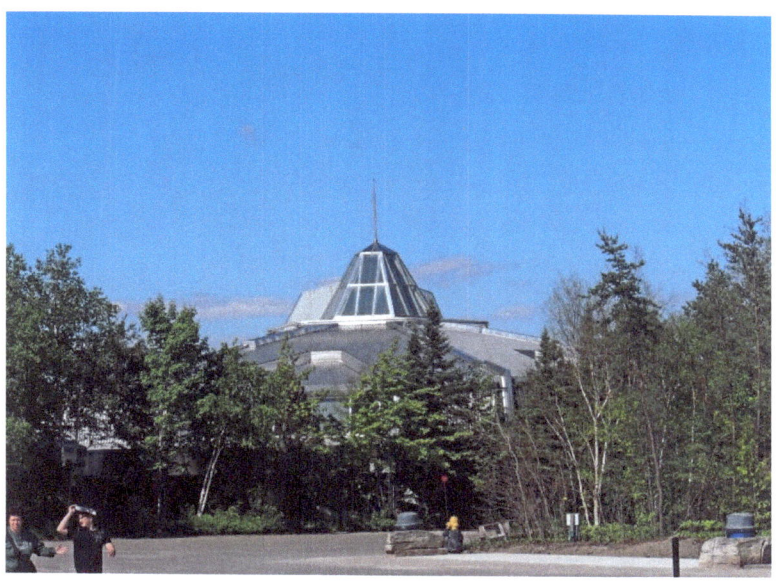

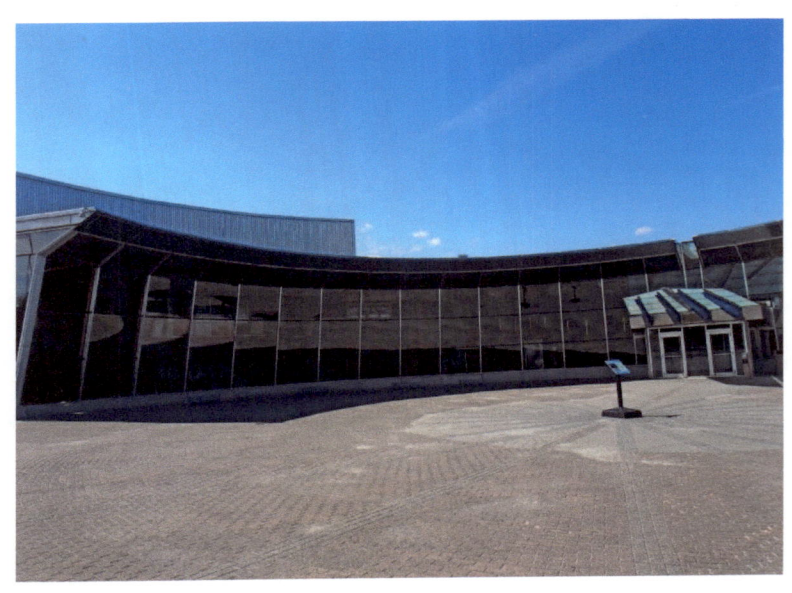

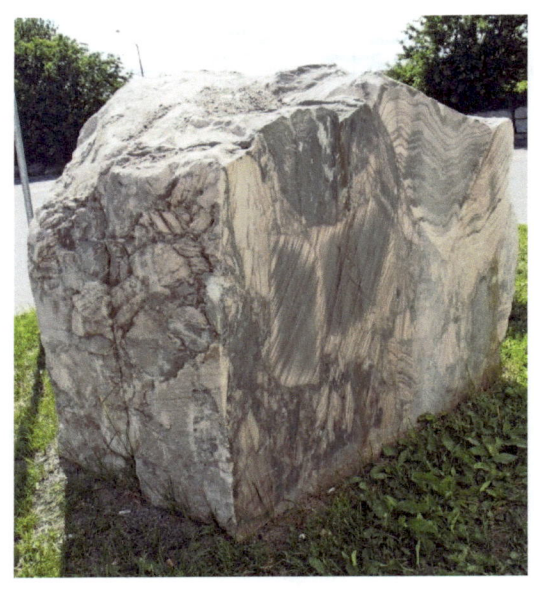

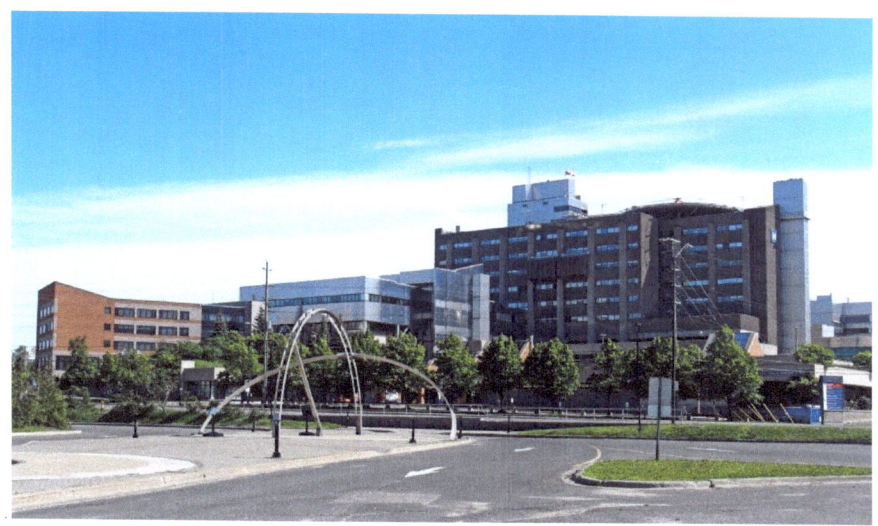

Hospital

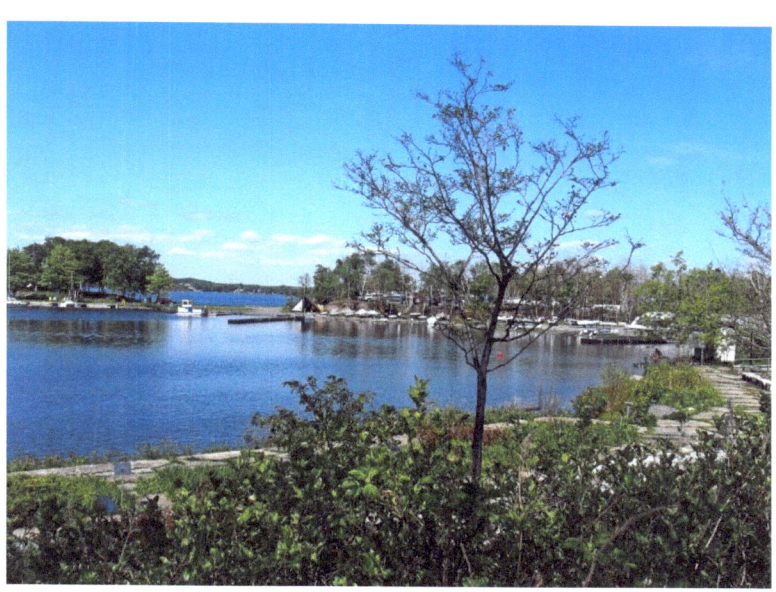

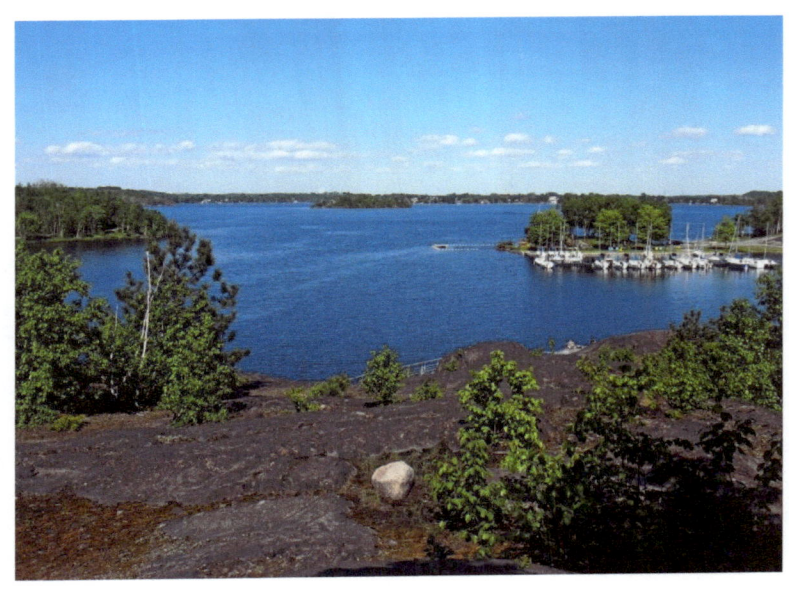

Ramsey Lake

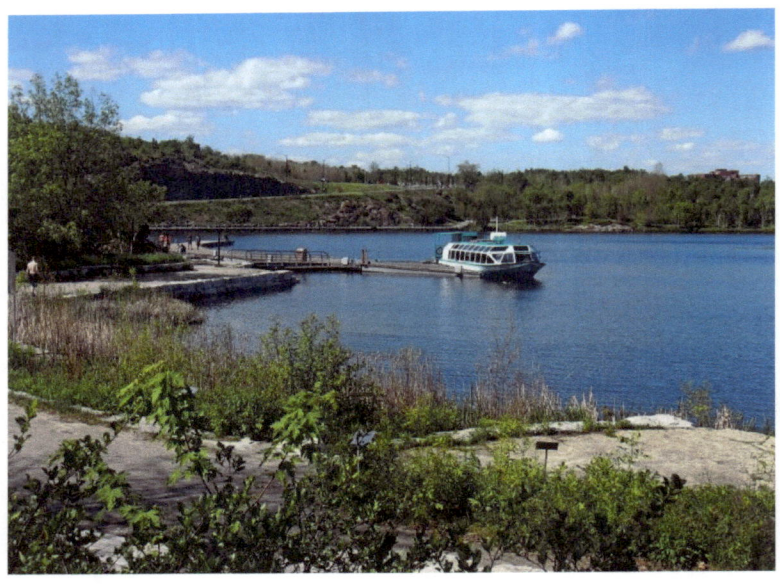

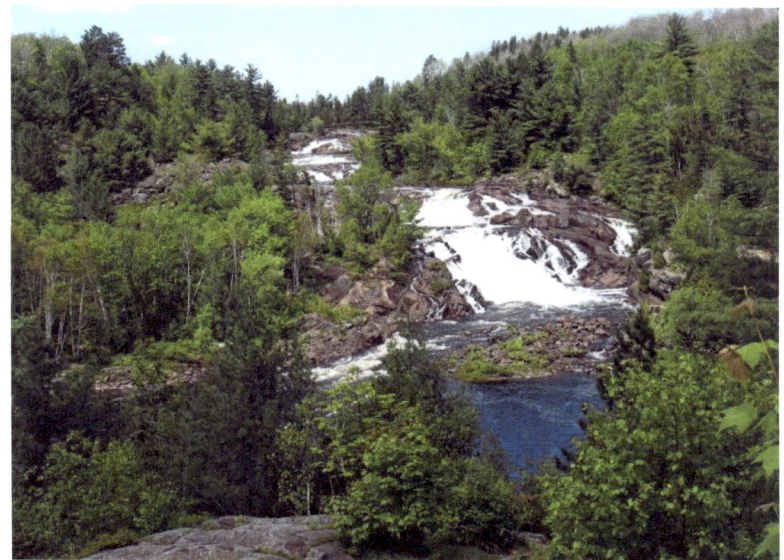

High Falls on the Onaping River drops 46 meters (150 feet) – In 1953 A.Y. Jackson, one of the founding members of the Group of Seven, painted "Spring on the Onaping River."

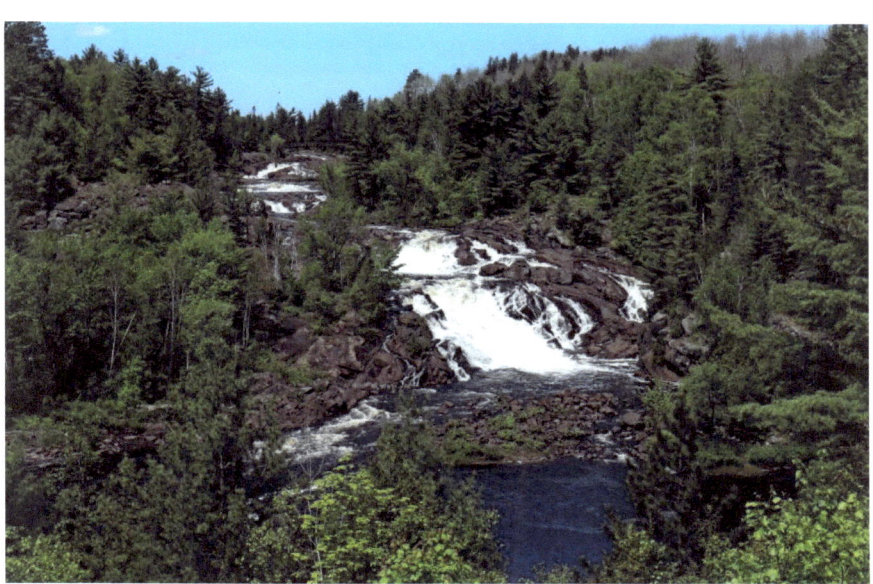

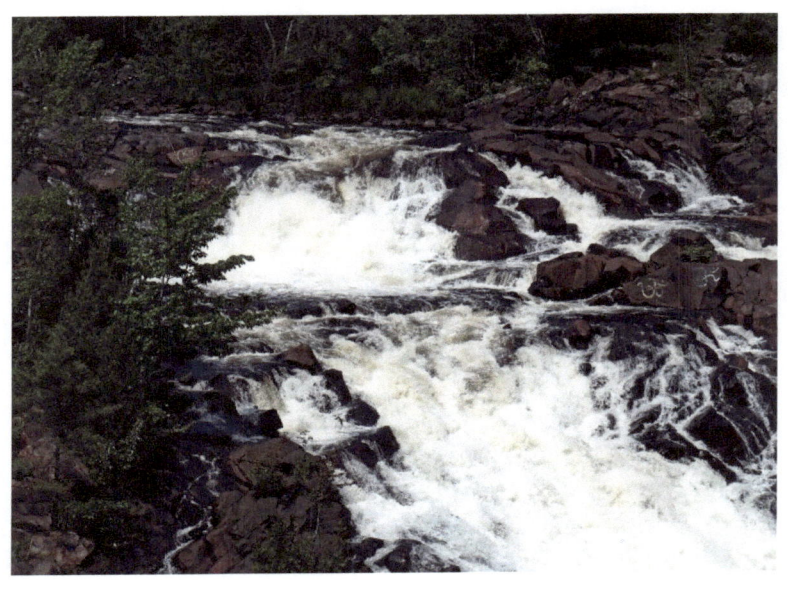

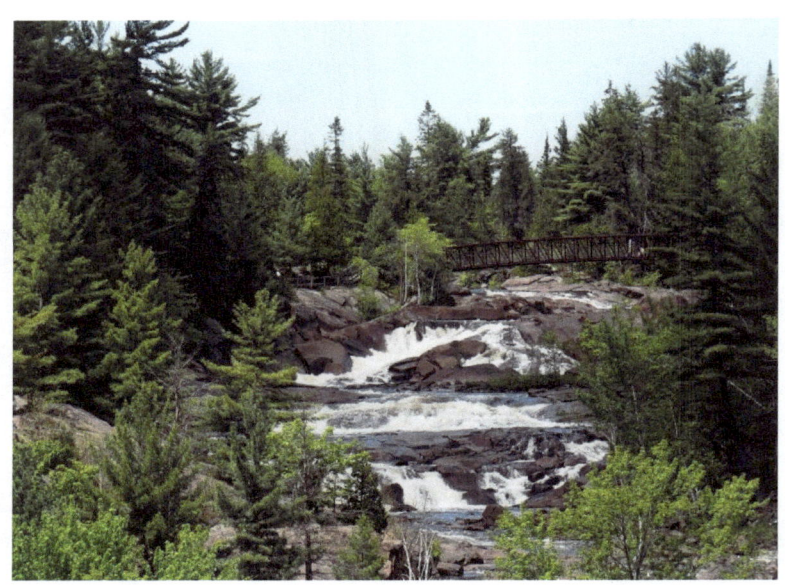

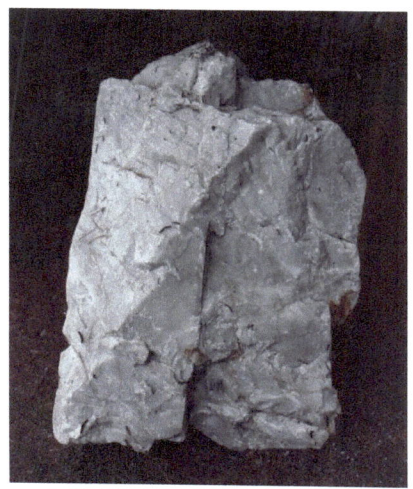

Quartzite from Inco's Lawson Quarry in Willisville near Whitefish Falls which operated from 1942 to 1980s – The silica in this pure quartz rock body (SiO_2) replaced the use of sand as the main converter flux at the Copper Cliff and Coniston smelters. The introduction of this silica rich rock reduced the volume of slag produced and lowered the slag metal loss content.

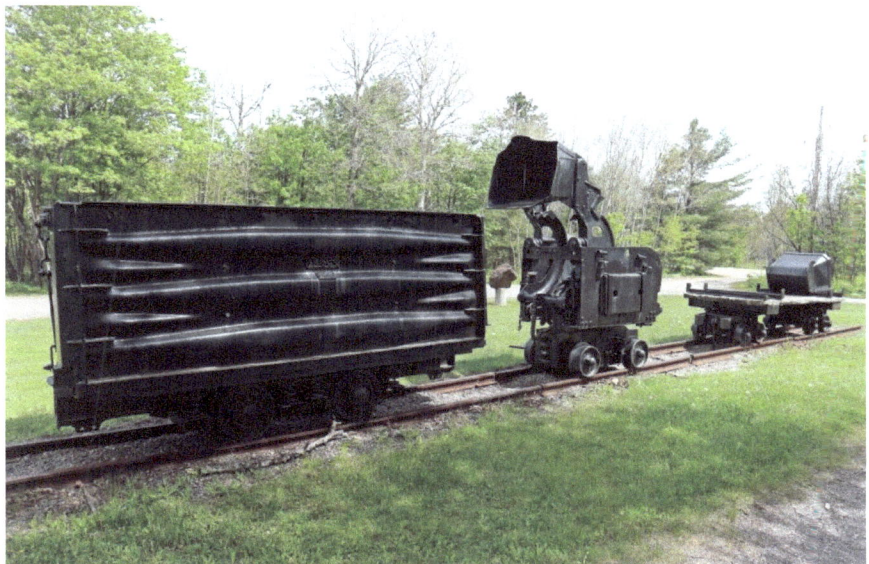

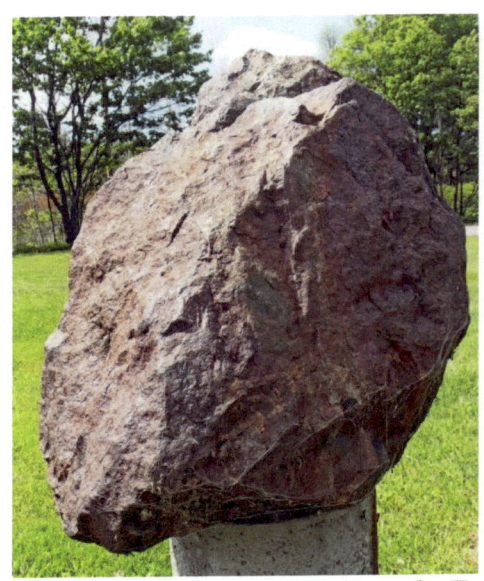

Granite Breccia from Inco's McCreedy East Mine

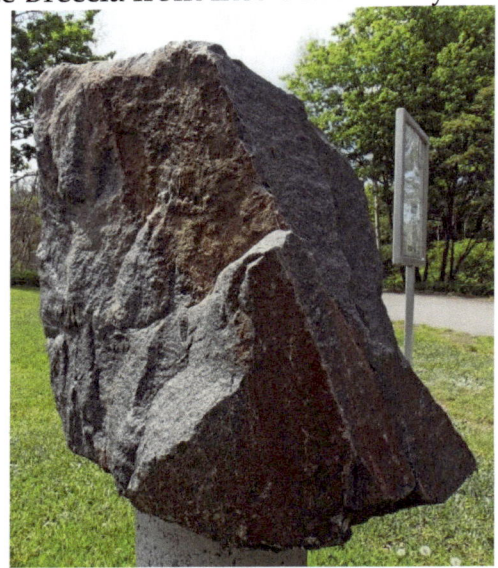

Norite – medium-coarse crystalline, Igneous-textured rock consisting mostly of plagioclase (white feldspar mineral) and dark pyroxenes. This mineral composition gives norite a salt and pepper appearance.

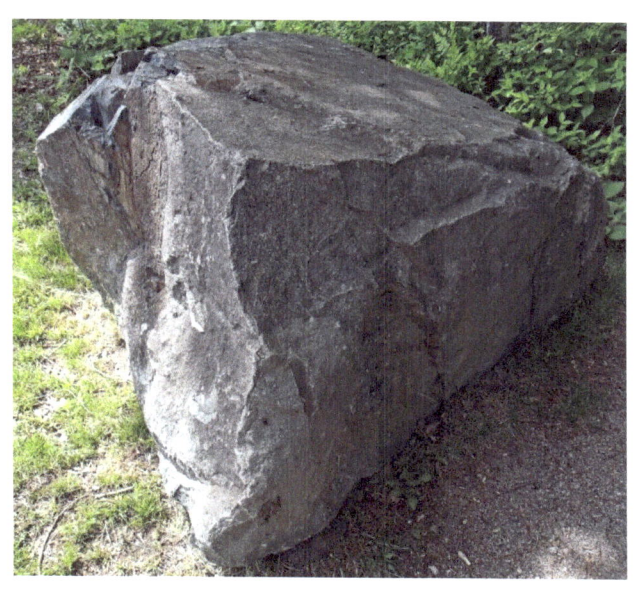

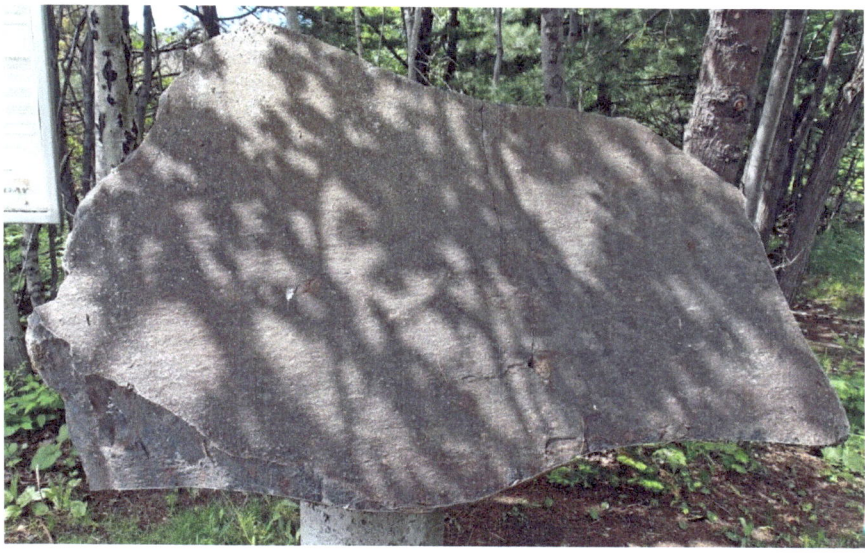

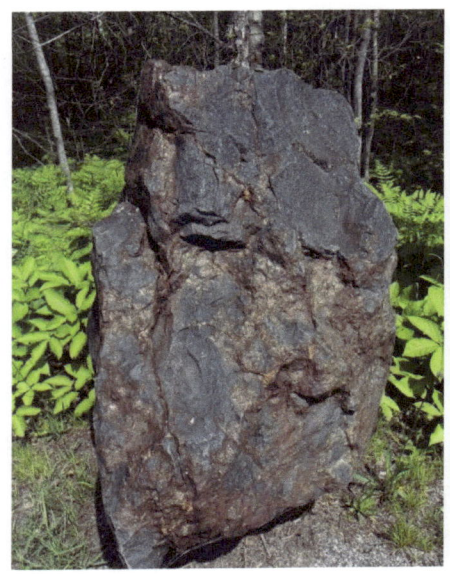
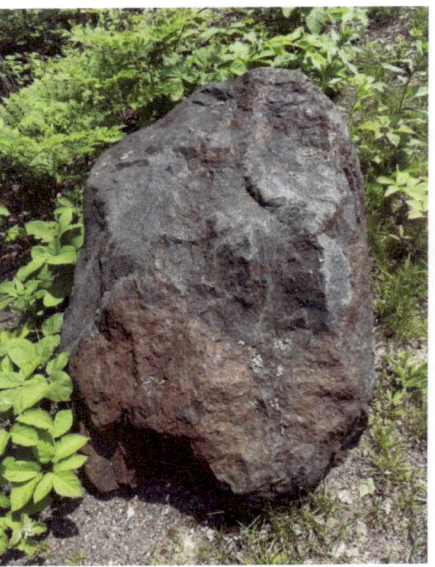
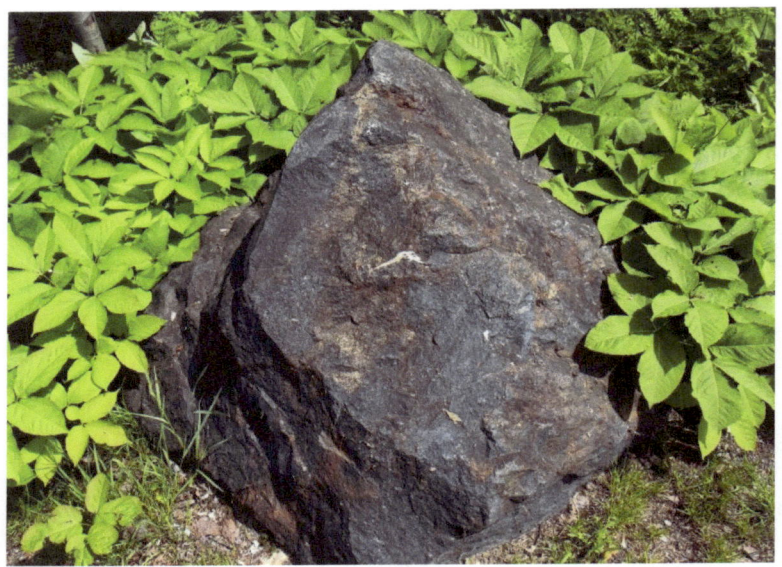

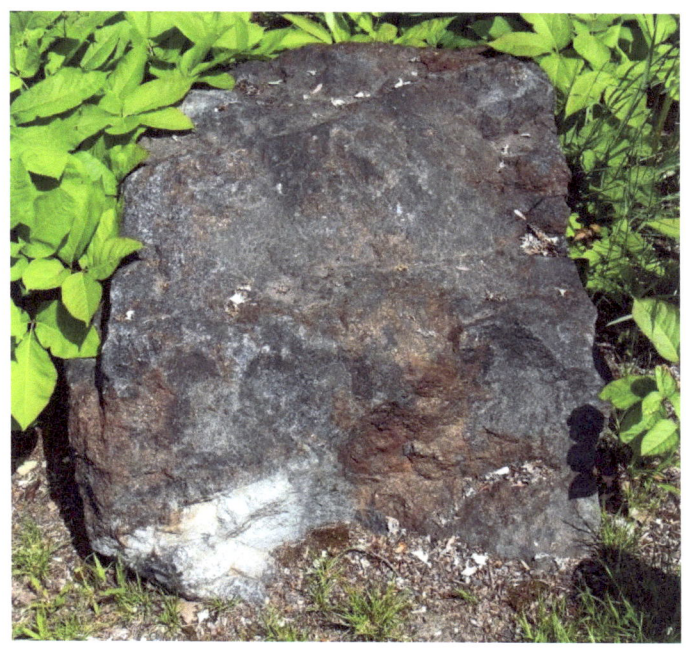

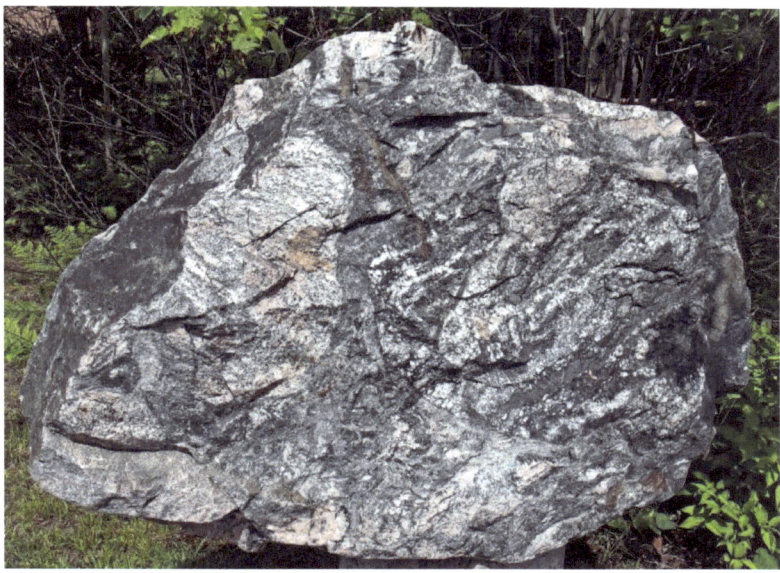

Breccia is rock consisting of angular fragments of older rocks cemented together.

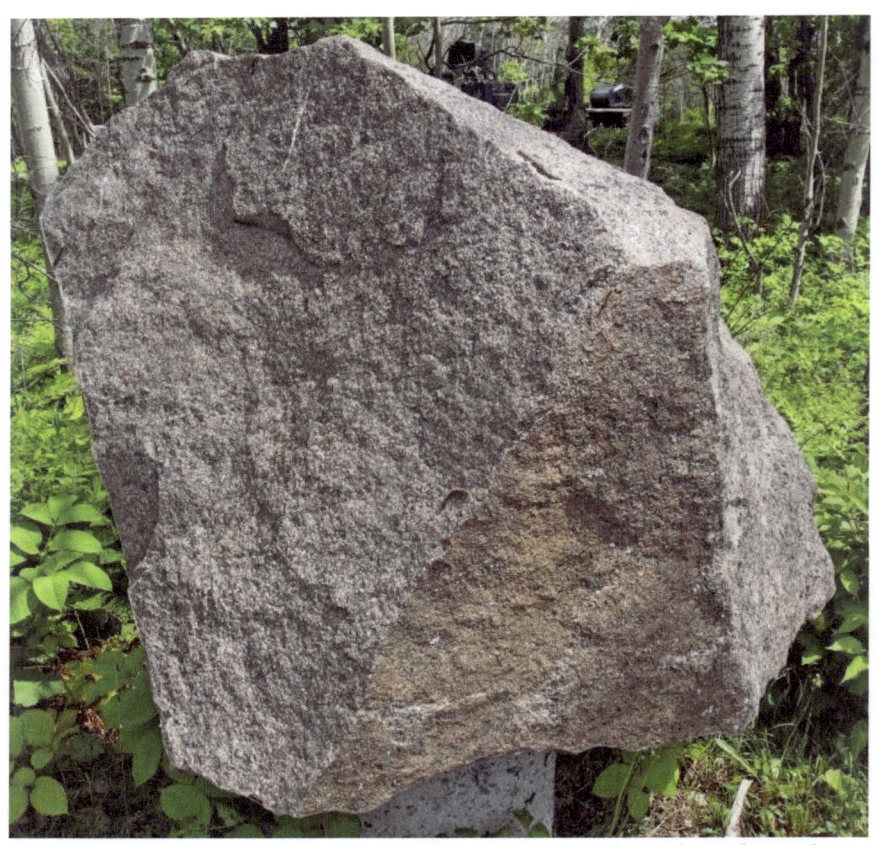

Granophyre is a distinctively pinkish colored rock with interlocked wedge-shaped quartz and feldspar crystals with plagioclase feldspar and minor amounts of biotite, amphibole, chlorite and opaque minerals.

Other Books by Barbara Raue

Coins of Gold
Arrows, Indians and Love
The Life and Times of Barbara
The Cromwell Family Book
Laura Secord Discovered
Daddy Where Are You?

Montana Series
Book 1: Montana Dream
Book 2: Life on the Montana Frontier
Book 3: Montana to Boston and Back
Book 4: Montana Sons Go to War
Book 5: Montana Sons Return from War

Visit Barbara's website to view all of her books
http://barbararaue.ca

© 2018 by Barbara Raue - All the photos in this book have been taken with my cameras. I own the rights to them.

www.ingramcontent.com/pod-product-compliance
Lightning Source LLC
Chambersburg PA
CBHW040232220526
45473CB00001B/217